SEEKING FOR
THE KINGDOM OF GOD

SANNERZ: "SUNHEART CHILDREN'S COMMUNITY"

Watercolor by Else von Hollander, Sannerz, 1924

SEEKING FOR
THE KINGDOM OF GOD

Origins of the Bruderhof Communities

by

Eberhard and Emmy Arnold

Selected and Edited from Earlier Sources
and Memories

by

Heini and Annemarie Arnold

PLOUGH PUBLISHING HOUSE

Hutterian Society of Brothers

Rifton, New York

1974

Originally prepared in 1973 for a
circular letter
Bible passages are translated from
the German as quoted by
Eberhard Arnold and Emmy von Hollander
unless otherwise acknowledged

Library of Congress Cataloging in Publication Data

Arnold, Eberhard, 1883–1935.
    Seeking for the Kingdom of God.

    "The writings and letters of Eberhard and Emmy
Arnold were translated from the original German and
edited by the Society of Brothers at Rifton, New York."
    1. Arnold, Eberhard, 1883–1935. 2. Arnold, Emmy.
3. Bruderhof Communities. I. Arnold, Emmy. II. Title.
BX8129.B68A684 1974   289.7'092'2 [B]   74–6317
ISBN 0-87486-133-0

Printed at the Plough Press
Hutterian Society of Brothers, Farmington, PA, U.S.A.

In Emmy Arnold's ninetieth year, we wish to express our gratefulness that the beloved widow of Eberhard Arnold is still active as a member of the Woodcrest Community.

This is also the hundredth year of our dear Tante Clara Weber, one of the two living daughters of Christoph Blumhardt and granddaughters of Johann Christoph Blumhardt.

In 1874, seeking religious freedom, our Brothers called Hutterians migrated from Europe (where they lived in full community of goods) to Bon Homme, South Dakota. Here in North America, they established the Hutterian Church again.

In 1954 our Hutterian Society of Brothers from England and South America established their first community in the United States at Woodcrest, Rifton, New York.

To commemorate these anniversaries and centennials, we publish this book in great thankfulness to God in this year of 1974.

CONTENTS

Introduction   ix

I   The Youth of Eberhard Arnold   1

II   The Struggle for the Word and Life of God
From the Engagement Letters of
Eberhard Arnold and Emmy von Hollander   37

III Else von Hollander
   1 Eberhard Arnold on Her Development and
     Family Background   213
   2 Some Memories of the Arnold Children   216
   3 From a Letter to Eberhard Arnold   220
   4 Four Poems   223
   5 Confession of Faith   227

IV   Conclusion: Our Emerging Bruderhof Life
   1 What Has Become Important for Us in Jesus?   231
   2 Eberhard Arnold's Search for the Will of God   234
   3 The Expectation of a New Beginning   239
   4 How the Church Community Came Into Being   240
   5 Historical Parallels: Anabaptism,
     Zinzendorf and Others   245
   6 How Eberhard Arnold Came to the
     Baptizer Movement
   7 The Early Christian Witness Has Never
     Come to an End   252
   8 The Significance of the Blumhardts   257
   9 The Meaning of "Inner Light" and "God's Spirit"   267

V   Postscript: Further Developments in the Bruderhofs   273

INTRODUCTION

In June 1920 a small group of Christians from the *Neuwerk* ("New Work") movement began community life in the little village of Sannerz, Hesse, Germany, 35 miles northeast of Frankfort on the Main. In 1927, after a period of crisis and growth, the group acquired a small farm in the Rhön hills not far from Sannerz. They called their new settlement, initially about thirty adults and children, "Bruderhof" in memory of the many communal households of the Brothers known as Hutterians in Moravia in the 16th and early 17th centuries. Today, in 1974, this small beginning in Germany has grown to four larger community settlements of about one thousand adults and children in the United States and England.

Eberhard Arnold, one of the first seven members of the Sannerz and Bruderhof communities, visited the thirty communal colonies of the Hutterian Brothers in the U.S. and Canada in 1930–1931. During this time they became fully united. After a time of discord, turmoil, and separation in the fifties, this unity emerged again in Sturgeon Creek Colony, Headingly, Manitoba, on January 7, 1974, with the more than two hundred Hutterian colonies now existing. It was consummated during the visit of five Hutterian brothers to our three Bruderhofs in the East from January 28 to February 13, 1974. We of the Society of Brothers are deeply moved by this event and consider it a gift of God's infinite grace and mercy.

Any movement of the Spirit that has lost its original strength and clarity can find true renewal only by going back to its Source. This is why Eberhard Arnold collected texts originating from earliest Christianity after New Testament times: "For in the fire of first love, in the abundance of God's manifestations, the rich, primitive force of the early Christian spirit speaks to us once again."[1] When seeking a genuine and desperately needed rebirth for our own small movement, we too had to return to its true source: the New Testament and early Christianity. We also felt we had to go back to the actual beginnings of the Bruderhof itself and to the inner and outer events that preceded the founding of community in Sannerz.

It was a deeply stirring experience for all Bruderhof members, young and old, when during the last few years the nine volumes of Engagement Letters written by Eberhard Arnold and Emmy von Hollander during the years 1907–1909 were read in our meetings. We all felt how shaken Eberhard and Emmy and Emmy's younger sister Else von Hollander were by the living Word of God—both in the Old and the New Testament. It reached the innermost recesses of their hearts and changed their lives completely and radically. Eventually, the revolutionizing inner experiences of these early years led to the community beginnings of the early twenties.

In the present volume we want to show how Eberhard, Emmy, and Else were led from the revivalist movement—without sacrificing its God-given early Christian elements—to the Youth Movement and religious socialism before 1920;

[1] Eberhard Arnold, *The Early Christians* (Rifton, New York: The Plough Publishing House, 1970), p. 53.

then later how the nascent community of Sannerz and the Bruderhof was led to the Brothers known as Hutterians, who began their communities of life and work as part of the 16th-century revival of New Testament Christianity in the Baptizer ("Anabaptist") movement; and how important was the faith of the Blumhardts (Johann Christoph, 1805–1880, and Christoph, 1842–1919), with their struggle for Christ's victory over the powers of evil and darkness and their faith for His future Kingdom.

We also feel it important to share something of Else von Hollander's life as a testimony to the significant contribution she made: she was Eberhard and Emmy's closest friend and companion in the twenty-five years of their common search until her death in 1932.

The letters, writings, and transcripts of this volume are also meant as a call to all brothers and sisters everywhere, a call to all concerned people, in whatever group, Church, or land, who are committed to a keen and uncompromising search toward Christian discipleship in love and obedience to Jesus and the early Church. We seek unity among all men who want to be brothers in the Spirit of Jesus. With Jesus and the Holy Spirit leading us, we seek a renewal of the decision made by Eberhard and Emmy Arnold and Else von Hollander, expressed by Eberhard in his letter to Emmy on October 5, 1907: "Jesus will lead everything marvelously .... I simply rely on God and go His way, *not looking to right or left*."

In 1529, while he was in prison in Gmünden, Austria, Peter Rideman (the early Hutterian missionary, apologist, and Elder) wrote in his *First Confession of Faith*:

HOW WE MUST BUILD THE HOUSE OF GOD
AND WHAT THE HOUSE OF GOD IS

Now the first pillar of this House is the
pure fear of God as is written:
The fear of God is the beginning of wisdom.
Against this pillar beat the mighty wind and
damaging water of the fear of man . . . .
We must stand against this, however,
in the fear of God,
And fear God more than men.

In the more than 54 years of our life in community the destructive power of the fear of man has tried to overwhelm us again and again. True community as the House of God must be firmly built on rock. That is why Jesus, our most beloved Master and Savior, says so clearly at the end of His Sermon on the Mount:

'What then of the man who hears these words of mine and acts upon them? He is like a man who had the sense to build his house on rock. The rain came down, the floods rose, the wind blew, and beat upon that house; but it did not fall, because its foundations were on rock. But what of the man who hears these words of mine and does not act upon them? He is like a man who was foolish enough to build his house on sand. The rain came down, the floods rose, the wind blew, and beat upon that house; down it fell with a great crash.'

When Jesus had finished this discourse the people were astounded at his teaching; unlike their own teachers he taught with a note of authority.   (Matt. 7:24–29, NEB)

Eberhard Arnold was born on July 26, 1883, in Königsberg, East Prussia. He spent most of his childhood and early youth in Breslau, Silesia, where his father Carl Franklin Arnold—born in Springfield, Ohio, in 1853, the son of an American missionary—was professor of Church history at the Friedrich-Wilhelm University.

The first chapter of this volume consists of Eberhard's own account of his early youth and conversion, the radical change he experienced as a 16-year-old grammar-school boy. This happened soon after he had visited his uncle Ernst Ferdinand Klein in Lichtenrade near Berlin in the summer of 1899. Uncle Ernst was a pastor who stood up for the poor and with all his spontaneity and humor represented a genuine, truly committed Christianity, which made a deep impression on young Eberhard. In this account, which Eberhard wrote probably in 1918 for his wife Emmy and his children, he gave himself the pseudoynm "Erhard." We replaced this with his true name throughout.

When Eberhard Arnold studied theology in Halle in 1907, he was secretary of the local Student Christian Movement and took an active part in the revival meetings, which hit the upper classes of Halle like a storm. This revival arose largely through the lectures given by Ludwig von Gerdtell, a radical evangelist and a lawyer by profession, who put the nature of the early Christian Church sharply into focus in modern language. He put his finger on the crying contrast between the faith and life of first-century Christianity and the false Church piety of his time. It was under the impact of this revival that Eberhard Arnold became acquainted with Emmy von Hollander in a Bible class he was holding at the residence of Mrs. Baehr, wife of the Surgeon General. Eberhard and Emmy became engaged a short time later, on Good Friday, March 29, 1907.

At that time Emmy von Hollander was training as a nurse

with the Order of St. John in Salzwedel. She was born on December 25, 1884, in Riga, Russia, the second child of J. Heinrich von Hollander and his wife Monika, née Otto. The von Hollanders with their six children had emigrated to Germany in 1890, where at the time of Eberhard and Emmy's engagement Heinrich von Hollander taught law at the university in Halle. Traditionally Lutheran, the von Hollander family had played a leading role in the administration of Riga, the old Hanseatic city of German traders and merchants.

For the greatest part, the present volume contains excerpts from the first three volumes of Eberhard Arnold's and Emmy von Hollander's Engagement Letters, covering the period of March 30 to October 5, 1907, under the title "The Struggle for the Word and Life of God." The Arnold-von Hollander letters reveal the profound struggle for a genuine Biblical Christianity that was going on in Eberhard, Emmy, and her sister Else during that time, particularly in 1907 and 1908. They felt called more and more deeply to go the way of Jesus completely, accepting all its implications and consequences step by step as they became clear to them, "not looking to right or left." They experienced clearly what we of the Bruderhofs feel so deeply today, that Jesus promised to be with us and has been faithful to this promise in spite of our own unworthiness and unfaithfulness. "For where two or three are gathered in my name, there I am in the midst of them."

(Matt. 18:20, RSV)

The true beginning of the Bruderhof therefore was not at the time of the actual founding of the community in Sannerz in 1920. It goes back to the struggles and victories in Halle in the year 1907, when "two or three" were already gathered in

Jesus' name, and further back still to the fall of 1899, when Eberhard experienced the tremendous upheaval of his conversion. This had given a completely new direction to his life: from then on he felt a burning love to Jesus and decided to follow Him whatever the cost.

The first fruit of the inner recognitions and struggles of the year 1907 was the realization that the baptism of the early Church was one of repentance, conversion, and faith, the visible stepping-stone from the old life to the new. The consequence of this recognition was that Eberhard, Emmy, and Else rejected child baptism and the organized State Church, which involved a sharp break with the usual norms of middle-class Christianity. (At that time the world Churches in Germany, whether Catholic or Protestant, were State Churches administered by the Ministry of Churches and Education; the State collected the Church taxes, and the pastors and ministers were State officials.) This brought them into painful conflicts with their families in Breslau and Halle, both in different ways so traditionally Protestant. Eberhard was not even allowed by the Board of Examiners (State Church officials) to sit for his final divinity exams. He dropped theology and studied philosophy and pedagogics instead, writing his doctor's thesis on the subject of the "Original Christian and Anti-Christian Elements in Friedrich Nietzsche's Development." This prolonged his studies for still one more year.

After receiving his degree in Erlangen in November 1909, Eberhard married Emmy on December 20, 1909, in Halle. They first lived in Leipzig, where Eberhard worked as an independent writer and lecturer, propagating the faith and life of early Christianity in close cooperation with Ludwig von

Gerdtell. Eberhard and Emmy moved from Leipzig to Halle in 1911 and from there to the mountains of Tyrol in 1913 and back to Halle at the outbreak of the First World War in 1914. Then in 1915 Eberhard became literary director of the Furche Publishing House in Berlin. At the same time he was editor of the magazine *Die Furche* ("The Furrow") and secretary of the German Student Christian Movement until the time the Bruderhof community began to take shape.

Emmy's sister Else von Hollander was born in Riga on December 13, 1885, and moved with her family to Germany at the age of four. From early childhood the two sisters were close friends, sharing their inner experiences and helping each other in their seeking. Else trained in an art school and made herself financially independent from her parents. In 1913 she joined Eberhard and Emmy in the Tyrol, working as Eberhard's secretary and helper. Later, because of her artistic talent and training, she was asked to be co-responsible for the layout and design of the Furche Publishing House books and art reproductions. These were outstanding in craftsmanship and design.

From these early years right to the time of her death on January 11, 1932, on the Rhön Bruderhof, Else von Hollander was inseparable from Eberhard and Emmy Arnold—with them she was committed to follow Jesus in joyful obedience and fellowship. Together they were seeking incessantly for a way of life more and more consistent with the life and teachings of Jesus. To this belonged the seeking of fellowship and full community with all those who were moved by the same Spirit that was at work in the early Church, with all those who were looking for a surrendered life of love in Jesus.

After the tremendous impact the life and message of Jesus made on Emmy, Else, and Eberhard in 1907, Else was the first to recognize some of the serious implications of the way of Jesus, the first to accept believer's baptism. To the horror and dismay of their parents and their eldest sister Olga, Emmy was the next to follow suit. A little later, Eberhard came to the same conviction independently, after serious consideration and thorough, deliberate study of the pertinent New Testament texts and early Church history. However, once this had become clear to him, there was no holding him back from obeying the commands of Jesus and the apostles whatever the consequences.

Nevertheless, he and Emmy felt that love to and respect for their parents demanded reasonable postponement of the actual steps of baptism and resignation from Church membership. They waited until 1908 to take these steps. To understand the attitude of the Arnold and von Hollander parents and relatives it must be realized that convinced German Protestants at that time, whether Lutheran or Reformed (the same was true of Catholics), regarded adult or believer's baptism and resignation from Church membership as tantamount to a complete rejection of all accepted, respectable religious values; for them it smacked of *Schwärmertum* ("religious fanaticism") and "Anabaptism," traditionally suspect of sedition and heresy by German Protestantism ever since the cruel massacre of 16th-century Anabaptists on the Continent. Hence the prolonged struggle of Eberhard, Emmy, and Else with both the von Hollander and Arnold parents, as is evident from the Engagement Letters. After all, Carl F. Arnold was a prominent Churchman in Silesia, and the von Hollanders were staunchly Lutheran in their whole outlook on life.

In the third chapter, the talk by Eberhard Arnold about Else von Hollander's family in 1932, as well as the words spoken by Hans-Hermann, Heini, Hardy, and Annemarie Arnold in 1972, were taken down verbatim in shorthand or recorded on tape. Everything said in these reports shows that the time before Sannerz (1907–1920) as well as the first eleven or twelve years of the community in Sannerz and on the Rhön are unthinkable without Else von Hollander. Her letter to Eberhard Arnold and her poems convey something of her dedication and deep spirituality. She was dearly beloved by all, adults and children, and is still unforgotten. Her adopted son Walter von Hollander lives in the community at Woodcrest with his family.

It is remarkable too that Monika von Hollander, who was drawn into the orbit of the Halle movement in 1907, also joined the community at Sannerz in the early years as a courageous cofighter. She married Georg Barth in 1927 and was a faithful sister to the end of her life in 1964. Georg and their three sons with their families belong to the Bruderhof communities in America.

Moreover, the eldest of the von Hollander sisters, Olga, so much in opposition to Emmy and Else during the revival in Halle, came to Sannerz in the fall of 1922 in the last stages of tuberculosis. She died peacefully in the warm, carrying atmosphere of love to Jesus prevailing in the community. Before she was called to Eternity she asked Eberhard Arnold and her sisters to take care of her adopted daughter Ruth after her death. Ruth lives now in the Woodcrest community with her husband Arno Martin and their youngest daughter.

It seems extraordinary that in this way all four surviving von Hollander children should have become a part of the growing community. At the time of writing only Emmy, Eberhard's widow (now in her 90th year), is still active as a member of the Bruderhof community at Woodcrest, New York.

The concluding chapter **IV**, "Our Emerging Bruderhof Life," contains selections from ten talks and discussions of Eberhard Arnold during the years 1932 to 1935 on the Rhön Bruderhof in Germany and on the Alm Bruderhof in Liechtenstein. They were all transcribed from shorthand notes with little or no amendment. They deal mainly with the different movements that contributed to the formation and inner growth of the community begun at Sannerz, of which the four Bruderhof communities in the U.S.A. and England are direct descendants.

Before and during the years of their residence in Berlin from 1915 to 1920, Eberhard, Emmy, and Else continued in their endeavor to live more in keeping with the life and teachings of Jesus. New aspects of truth were revealed by contemporary witnesses, for instance: Hermann Kutter, the Swiss Religious Socialist; the Blumhardts; Wassil Rachoff, the late 19th-century follower of Jesus in Russia; Leo Tolstoi; and Gustav Landauer, the prophetic anti-Marxist communitarian Socialist.

In 1918–19 Eberhard came to a decisive encounter with the Free German Youth movement. Here was a freshness of spirit, an honesty and openness for a new, genuine life style, which was truly astounding. From the joining of genuine elements from the revivalist movement, religious socialism, and the Youth Movement, the *Neuwerk* Movement came into being in Berlin and Hesse in 1919 and led to the beginnings of the small community at Sannerz in 1920.

In sections 1–4 of chapter IV an outline is given of movements and events bearing on Eberhard's inner development and that of his friends and associates in Berlin during and immediately after the First World War. They tell of some of the experiences that led this small, concerned circle to a life in full community. Sections 5 and 6 show the common search of the group in Sannerz and on the Rhön Bruderhof for similar movements of communitarian life in the 16th, 18th, and 19th centuries with particular emphasis on Zinzendorf and the Hutterian Brothers of the Baptizer Movement.

In section 6 Eberhard also shows how the almost exclusive emphasis on the Pauline Epistles characteristic of the revival movement shifted later to an emphasis on the Gospels, in particular on the Sermon on the Mount, embracing all of life's aspects: "We had a vision of a life that was one whole unity . . . of religion, economy, and justice."

During his journey to America in 1930–31, Eberhard Arnold spent many months with the Hutterian Brothers in South Dakota, Manitoba, and Alberta; and the small community on the Rhön became fully united with them. Eberhard also made short visits to the Inspirationist communities in Amana, Iowa, and to the Doukhobors in western Canada.

In section 7 of the last chapter Eberhard Arnold speaks of the innermost significance of the Hutterian conception of Christian life. "That alone is justification when the whole life of Jesus is planted and unfolded in us anew," and "faith . . . has to become active in love; it has to manifest itself as complete unity of work and life." That is why the Bruderhof united with the Hutterian Brothers.

Section 8 deals with the significance of Johann Christoph and his son Christoph Blumhardt for the emerging community life: Where Jesus is at work, Satan goes to the attack. A fight of spirits ensues in which Jesus is victorious. This is what the Blumhardts experienced as a powerful struggle for the victory of Jesus, waged by them in faith and hope and in ardent expectancy of God's Kingdom on earth.

The last section of the fourth chapter points to the universal, cosmic perspectives of God's creation and its redemption in Jesus, showing us the infinitesimal smallness of man and the earth in the vast universe and the overpowering, tremendous greatness of God and His Kingdom.

Woodcrest   *Hardy Arnold*
1974

I   THE YOUTH OF EBERHARD ARNOLD

I THE YOUTH OF EBERHARD ARNOLD

This is Eberhard Arnold's account about his background, his rebirth at the age of 16 in 1899, and his seeking to follow Jesus to the end.

The promenade was alive with people. Many schoolboys from the Holy Spirit Secondary School, from John's Grammar School, and from several other schools met there. Only a few knew each other. The girls, who came from the girls' high schools and colleges, were little heeded. Only now and again one of the boys said something nasty about one or the other of the girls, and indeed, the more impossible it seemed to his more naive comrades, the more certainly and definitely he insisted that it was true.

When the boys said good-bye, they spoke hurriedly and casually about this or that piece of homework so as to deal more thoroughly with the chief thing, which was their meeting in the afternoon.

Two meeting places vied for acceptance. One was Kurt Krone's garden, where they used to shoot at sparrows with a rifle and where real student rapiers could be got from his brother. It was true; they really fenced with these and enthusiastically tried all kinds of different passes. Blows and commands were carefully practiced. Of course, when it came to a real fight, these thirteen-year-old boys did not use sharp swords, but still, with well-made canes as foils, the blows hurt more than many a student wound that came from an almost imperceptible small cut in the skin. The great excitement was certainly not less with this cane-duelling than with the dangerous rapier-duelling of the university students. "To swords!" They stood ready. "Cross your swords!" "Ready!" "Go!" Blows fell to and fro right to the end. All that happened in deep seriousness and with burning enthusiasm.

The other meeting place of the eighth graders was less typically student and unfortunately less innocent. There was a secret entrance to a "cave" in Otto Wolf's garden, beneath the summer arbor. Quite a good part of this small garden had been dug out underneath. Down underground even the smallest boys had to stoop quite low to move on in. The whole construction allowed little room for movement. Only two or three or at the most four or five could go into the cave. Here there was a great deal of smoking and drinking. Still worse things took place secretly, about which nobody was allowed to know. The upright and uncontaminated boys got to hear of this filth only through hints meant to make them regret they were still ignorant of what was going on. Yet in spite of being openly despised by the others, these boys did not want to know anything about such activities. They had enough of it by only looking once into that dark and mysterious cave. So too on this day about which we are concerned, Eberhard Arnold, Kurt Krone, and Paul Schrenk did not want to have anything at all to do with these things. They remained foreign and hateful to them. When Otto Wolf hinted darkly about what would be taking place that day underground, their only answer was a calm and imperturbable silence. Finally, when Otto obviously did not want to go home with him over Lessing Bridge, Paul became irritable and impatient. With a violent movement, which had nothing to do with his words, Paul shouted loudly at him that at the moment he had something else to talk about. So the three friends were happily rid of the secretive Wolf. Yet it was clear from his whole behavior how furious he was from the snub he had received. "I know exactly how his face looks now. I can just see his angry look," Kurt said to his friends as they looked at their hurriedly retreating comrade. "He'll never forgive us for that. He's a coward, like all such people, and hates us just like a real wolf."

Nevertheless the three did not allow themselves to be distracted for very long. They talked in detail about the strict regulations of the new Suevia Club and agreed on the date of the next fencing practice. Their bright blue, white, and pink ribbons were proudly shown. The more severely the school threatened to punish them for their forbidden clubs, the more the boys were attracted by the romanticism of this otherwise so distant life of the university students; they felt they had to get to know about it and experience it already in their boyhood. Especially Kurt (the son of a well-to-do furniture manufacturer) was happy that his brother could belong to the Borussia Student Union, a club that was allied to the Bonn Borussians —that is to say, it really ranked as the poshest club or student organization in the whole city. At the bottom of his deeply yearning heart, Kurt was not so vain and stupid as would often appear from his loud boasting and the very overbearing way in which he told about his brother's twenty pints of beer a day and high monthly allowance. The eighth graders had not yet got past the most childish period of boasting to each other. One of them could tell about a certain magnificently bred and exquisitely groomed black horse (which actually belonged to the neighbor) as though this noble steed belonged to his parents; finally he almost believed this audacious swindle himself. Another comrade with a rather wild appearance declared quite seriously that his father was the Russian Czar, who had sent him there to receive a German grammar school education, which was superior to that obtainable in Russia. He could describe this remarkable fate in a moving way, and concluded his detailed account usually with the simple words, "And so that I should not be too conspicuous among you, my father, the Czar, gave me for life the simple German name of *Knopf* ('Button')." The eighth graders wanted to be great and famous and to glory in unheard-of riches and the mightiest of privileges.

Eberhard and Paul Schrenk realized that a quiet and hidden transformation was taking place within them, which was alienating them more and more from these activities. They belonged to the Suevia Club for only a few weeks. Only once had they both got drunk and tried in vain to walk straight along the cracks between the paving stones, asking all passers-by for a herring to overcome their drunkenness. Of course at home a much more effective medicine awaited them: a beating. But it was neither this nor the severe school punishment that gave them the strength to break away from this wrong path on which they had just started. Rather it was the unspeakable emptiness of this pleasure and the indescribable disgust that had lodged itself in them. It was the untruthfulness of this boasting that they met everywhere—in parties given at their parents' houses, in the student circle of their older brothers, and now in their own boyish life at school, in the public street, and behind every window. It was this disgust that drove them out of all this confusion and forward, without their knowing in what direction a new way would lead them.

So today both looked in each other's eyes a moment longer than they would have done without this experience. They shook hands so hard that weaker boys would have cried out. Then suddenly Paul ran without stopping past the Government Building toward Lessing Bridge. In this way he escaped any further emotional outburst—also his mother (who came from Oldenburg and was very proud of her family connections) knew how to reprove any unpunctuality for lunch without many words but in a most embarrassing way.

Eberhard Arnold strode out with a long step past Holtey Hill toward the old upper class house in which his father, a scholarly, high-ranking Church official, had taken up his residence two years before.

No agreeable family life awaited Eberhard at home. His father preferred to be in his office or in his study. It was not unusual for him to get up from a meal, while everyone else was eating, to withdraw in an irritable mood (sometimes during breakfast with his cup full of coffee). A sharp word from his wife or a clumsy remark from one of his five children had hurt or provoked him; it pained him to say so, but it was his verdict on his own family that they lacked intellectual interests. Then in his large room, bowed down over the Prophets of his old Bible, he would strive for self-composure, often in vain. Sometimes he would return during the mealtime with a forced and friendly smile, but a friendlier atmosphere in the dining room was not achieved. How gladly would he have given his family the deep peace that he so often, with furrowed brow, implored God to give him. His faith appeared to spread more torment than joy.

Certainly in his way he loved all his children, just as he preserved a passionate affection for his wife Elizabeth right into old age; but he did not succeed in expressing this love convincingly. Even though he energetically represented the best aspects of the Protestant Church, and even though it was his wish that serious Christianity penetrate all the cultural activities of the city, yet his keen irony often appeared to show more a despising of men, rather than a love that witnessed to a faith in Christ as reality. At home, it is true, he took on humble services gladly, even though the generously managed household in no way needed his help. Yet his efforts seemed to come from a certain asceticism or self-humiliation, by means of which he tried to master himself and others. Perhaps his origin and education played a part in determining his behavior.

As a result of the revival under Charles Finney, Eberhard's great-grandfather, (an American farmer) had sent his son, Eberhard's grandfather, to take up theology and become a Puritan missionary and pastor. Eberhard's grandmother came from the educational circle which had gathered round Heinrich Pestalozzi in German Switzerland. Her family developed into a powerful line of pastors and educators in one of the small German States. Branches of this family served in rural parishes as simple tutors and at times also as teachers at the courts of princes. Eberhard's father thought about all these things

without pride. They seemed to fill him with a humiliating consciousness of bourgeois dependence and servility to the princes,
the educational results of which were to him more than question-
able, especially in Russia. When Eberhard's father was a small
boy, he had come to live in an upper class house in one of the
Hanseatic cities [Bremen] because of the unfavorable climate
in Africa, his parents' mission field. This upper class house
was noted for its intellectual and material wealth. For people
who were not professional scholars, his foster parents and their
relatives possessed an unusually profound philosophical and
theological education. At times their family played a leading
role in the foremost society circles of the big Hanseatic city.
They took an earnest and often determining part in Church
life. Wealth was available for Eberhard's father's education.
As the child of missionaries he found all this depressing. Instead
of it giving him more courage for life, it led him to an often
tormenting humility and shyness. This was an unusual contrast
to his pride and superiority as a scholar. His foster parents'
pietism and biblicism was like that of Collenbusch,[1] broadened
and refined in bourgeois society, but it did not become his
spiritual inheritance even though what Collenbusch taught
him about life never left him. The oppressive greatness and
strictness of the Old Testament seemed to influence him more
deeply than the loving, healing depths of God's heart in the
New Covenant.

The jolly and at that time still morally steady life of young
university students had only temporarily a youthful and en-
livening influence on him. At the end of his years of study,

[1] Devotional biblicist (1724–1803), forerunner of Gottfried Menken (see
p 12).

the apostolic and spiritual radicalism of a non-Church community came close to bringing him decisive help. But on the
advice of a leading Churchman, this most inwardly challenging
awakening was directed into the tranquilizing channels of the
Moravian Church, which already then had become very soft
and compromising. Just at this period of his inner life, he made
acquaintance with his beloved Elizabeth's parents' home. She
was the proud and beautiful daughter of one of his university
professors in theology. He belonged to the most orthodox and
morally strict direction but unfortunately lacked the gift of
passing on his strict faith to his five children. Perhaps the
firmness of his confession lacked that deep glow of mystical
inwardness that was given to his more famous father-in-law
(a star in the firmament of the world of learning—only a few
outshone him as his only brother did, one of the well-known
authorities on ancient Greece). Both Eberhard's great-grandfather Julius[2] and his brother came from an old Lutheran
pastor family from the southeast of the German world. They
had an influence on Eberhard's inner life, an influence that
had come down and was in no way weakened throughout the
almost one hundred years' span of time.

Eberhard's grandfather had married one of the seven daughters of this ancestor, Julius. She was a tender woman with a
fine feeling but as much a stranger to true life and its needs
as her extremely serious husband. She hardly ever set her foot
on the streets of her university town. Her habit of going around
in a hackney carriage was well-known in the city. Neither she
nor her husband devoted themselves to the upbringing of their

[2] Julius Müller (1801–1878).

children. It belongs to the mysteries of such families, who had been endowed with the Christian faith for generations, that in spite of this lack of care, four of them achieved something and were successful in life. Three were respected representatives of the scholastic, artistic, and higher civil servant class. The fourth was the mother of our Eberhard and his four brothers and sisters. The youngest daughter, whose pampered beauty was surrounded by so much vanity, later brought much unhappiness to the family. For all her brothers and sisters, and not the least for Eberhard's parents, this family suffering was very hard for them all their lives, lasting even after this unhappy youngest daughter had died in a mental asylum. She had been taken there more to protect the good name of the family than for her own benefit. The family, so proud of the great number of scholarly ancestors and relatives, tried to see the guilt for this misfortune as inherited from the grandfather on the father's side. This great-grandfather of Eberhard was a simple master craftsman whose son, it is true, had managed to become a university professor and high Church official. His granddaughter was supposed to have inherited her bad character from him. Whether there was enough reason to think so must be quite seriously doubted. At any rate one thing is certain, that with the other four children of this Church official, in spite of their high moral attitude to life (which lasted right into old age), their upbringing had emotional consequences; their upbringing was not able to lead them to a true life because it gave it too little guidance.

At first the newly married couple (Eberhard's parents), were happy. Their first years of married life in the city where he held office passed without grave disturbance. Eberhard's father ascended slowly and surely the ladder of his career, thanks to his rich and all-embracing education. When Eberhard was five years old, his father was called to Breslau, another large city. Eberhard had only a few memories of his birthplace: that once he had broken through the ice into the frozen river and was brought home wet and cold, that he had looked down into the mirror behind a cobbler's cellar door, and that his maternal grandfather wore a top hat. He had more recollections of the wealthy house of his other grandfather in the Hanseatic city where his father grew up. There, when he was a small boy, he had listened through an old-fashioned speaking tube up on the top floor and heard the murmur of the huge party that was in the reception rooms on the first floor below. At that time a jolly old uncle had pointed out to the children what confusion would arise if they were to mix up all the twenty pairs of galoshes. Quickly Eberhard and the other children set about the mischief. Late at night they listened through the speaking tube to all the noise of the guests. It took a long time before each one had the right pair of galoshes. To this day Eberhard can see the strict and firm eyes of his grandmother, long since dead, as she looked at him; her exhortations were extremely impressive.

Little Eberhard had certainly innumerable recollections of the time when he was five and six years old and lived in the city that was the new and final sphere of his father's activities. His governess (who appeared to him to be very old) was dreadful. She liked giving him a box on the ears when his arithmetic or writing did not sink in quickly enough. In that respect the first grade at school was much better. Even the

painful remembrances of the cane, which whistled down onto
the calf of his leg to the rhythm of the words, "That is your
first caning," was better than being boxed on the ears by the
horrid old governess. Little Eberhard never forgot how the
heavy first grade teacher imitated his way of running and
taught him that one should never be so stupid as to run after
other children who are up to some mischief if one has no idea
of what it is all about oneself.

Eberhard could talk over all his experiences with Adalbert
Fischer, a son of the Post Office Director and a fine lad. How
heavy the separation was when Fischers were moved to another
post office! To whom could Eberhard tell now all he saw and
felt so strongly? For the first time he experienced the atmosphere around each person as he passed them by in the street. It
seemed to him that each one left behind him an invisible, but
nevertheless very potent web of influences, a dangerous extension of his being, which appeared to be exactly the same
size as his figure. It was horrible to have to go through such
a filled atmosphere when he had to cross the path of another.
What a disgusting stream is so often left behind by certain
people, even from the most fleeting encounter.

His mother exercised the strongest influence over him. Her
eyes (which saw almost everything) possessed something very
compelling. In spite of continually renewed protests, his scholarly father had long since left the management of the household to his practical wife. She considered him very much out
of place in all family affairs. "You should have been a monk,"
she used to say. She was often excited and irritable. In spite
of her husband's quite good salary and the property his foster
parents gave him, Eberhard's mother had to make great efforts

to manage the household economy with two servant girls. With sacrificial industry, she sewed and stitched till midnight. Only then would she look for the often misplaced newspapers and magazines, which then were probably her only recreation. There was family worship; but apart from their father himself, who read from old sermons, nobody listened to the "endless Menken."[3]

It seems that also many other intellectual efforts on the part of their father found no echo in the family. However, the reading of Goethe's "Magic Apprentice" by the weak light of a silver gray paraffin lamp, hung high up on the wall of the children's room, did leave an unforgettable impression. This work could have been a perpetual warning to children regarding relations with demonic powers. But when their father read "Götz von Berlichingen," by the same great poet in the same dimly-lit children's room, the children dreamed away the time without being able to understand the plot or its importance, for most of the five still did not go to school. Their father usually stood upon one leg with the other bent slightly sideways, resting on the tip of the toe. This was a typical attitude of his, which had earned him the nickname of "Stork" from other children. The same fruitless results came from learning long Psalms by rote. When little Eberhard was nine years old, he had himself chosen one of David's Psalms for reciting in front of the whole family. Without the others knowing, he chose (probably because of its shortness) one of David's Psalms of repentance, which shockingly confessed and openly revealed the young king's most terrible sins. Even his serious father could not prevent himself from bursting out into a laugh. The

[3] Gottfried Menken (1768–1831), pietist pastor and author in Bremen.

contrast between the sinful king and the completely innocent little boy was too great.

The intellectual talks of their father with his many guests at table, embracing the whole of cultural history and especially the 18th century and the time of Goethe in the 19th, were apparently little heeded by his own family. All the same, far more stimulation and competence to form an opinion came to them from this intellectual atmosphere than they could guess then. The scathing verdict of their father on the dullness and spiritual monotony of the cultural situation at that time (the end of the 19th century) sank deep into them. When they were older, under the influence of their philosophically well-educated father it became clearer to them that the deep Germanism of a Fichte, Schelling, or Schleiermacher, as also the inner heroism that was given to Carlyle and Macaulay, were hardly to be found in Germany anymore. "In the sense of a more elevated intellectuality, our day is extremely boring, and our politics are completely stupid, yes, fundamentally wrong, since Bismark's departure."

Eberhard's mother valued the intellectual education of his father highly without ever searching into its inner content. She was indignant, however, because in her opinion he did not know how to utilize his abundant knowledge to further the social and scholarly fame of the family, and thereby to further its economic ascent; and his father spoke still more despisingly of the shallow press reporters, of literary people, and of writers who knew how to whip up empty froth but never had the thoroughness to go back to the sources for their information.

What was most painful for him was that his wife, in spite of her theological background, had grave doubts concerning

the Christian faith. She made the reproach, often when the
children were present, that one could see too little joy and
certainty in her husband's sterile and anxiously conscientious
fight for faith. The inner fruitlessness of his spiritual fight
shocked and repelled her instead of winning her. The family's
regular going to Church soon exercised an anti-Church influence on Eberhard, because they would be quarreling amongst
themselves in the morning and then sit very solemnly in the
foremost Church pews. If it was at all possible, he left the
common family pew in the privileged part and climbed to the
highest point of the gallery to cut names in the Church pew
there or to read Karl May. He liked this author on account
of his fluent style and said of him, "He is so wild and so
religious at the same time."

Even his confirmation was not able to bring about any
change in him. When he was kneeling on the altar steps,
Eberhard, who was now becoming older, thought more about
his new adult suit (fixing his brilliant white cuffs at the last
minute so that they could be seen) than about the confession
demanded of him. Even then he was already angry over the
class distinctions. It angered him that he and his sister went
forward along with the other upper class children, he in a
black suit and she in a blazing white dress, while the poorer
boys in dark blue suits and the poorer girls in black dresses
had to follow on behind. When Eberhard realized that the
poorer families were not in a position like the richer ones to
buy a white evening dress for their girls in addition to the
necessary and always usable best black dress and that it was
the same with the boys, then in spite of his own vanity, he

had the irrefutable feeling that this way of doing things by the Church was unchristian.

From his thirteenth year on, Eberhard had strong doubts about the justice and truthfulness of the social and class distinctions to which he had been accustomed at home. In the mountains where he had spent his summers, he had discovered such a true humanity with so much heart among the country people that he could no longer have any sympathy for traditional class differences. One day he had sat down on the bench by the side of the front door of the small peasant cottage rented by his mother for the whole family as a holiday home and run by her with one of her servant girls. Eberhard was looking away at the far-distant high mountains when a tired old man, poorly dressed, stepped towards him and asked this child of a privileged class for some alms for his wanderings over hill and dale, from village to village, and from country to country. Eberhard still did not know the value of money, for he was always looked after and given everything his small life needed. He had seen a quarter of an hour earlier how the servant girl had peeled potatoes in the kitchen. He had been surprised at what a big sack of unpeeled potatoes had stood there. So he asked the wayfarer if he would like some potatoes, saying that in the kitchen there was a huge sack, which he with his parents and four brothers and sisters could not possibly eat up for a long time. The old man laughed and looked at the small boy who was so ignorant of the world with such astonished and kindly eyes that soon a very short but unforgettable friendship was formed between them. He sat down on the bench beside the boy, and the boy exchanged the old man's cap for his own summer hat. So the two sat for quite a time talking together, being silent together, and feeling happy together.

Suddenly Eberhard saw his mother standing near him with strict and shocked eyes. She asked in a sharp voice, "What kind of cap are you wearing? Go inside; I'm coming straight away." The old man stood up, embarrassed, and Eberhard's mother pressed a few pence into his hand, murmuring something about her stupid boy, and let the man go on his way. In the parlor of the mountain cottage there were hard words and hot tears. "How can you sit with a tramp and even put his cap on your head? Don't you know what you can have picked up?" The fine summer hat was burnt. Eberhard had to sit on a chair put carefully by itself in the middle of the room. His zealous mother wound a large white sheet around him and worked on his stupid little head with a sharp dandruff comb. Sure enough, the feared-for discovery was soon made. To his astonishment Eberhard's skull was shorn bare. Then he had to go straight to bed to think about his misdeed; but he could not grasp what wrong he had done, and his heart was with the wanderer and his kindly eyes. After that experience, Eberhard found it painful to let the servant girl attend him and to go on treating her so indifferently as if she were not a human being the same as he was, or as his brothers and sisters and his parents were.

From all outward signs, he appeared just as thoughtless as before. At school he worked little, for he lived under the constant illusion that as the son of his parents he could get on in the best schools without any special effort, and that he would advance to the higher positions in life just as effortlessly as he had benefited from the wealth and care of his parents' house. He dressed very carefully, loitered along the city's main street before supper, rowed on the river, learnt to swim, excelled in gym and football, visited the horse races with a proud yellow season ticket, and at fifteen or sixteen years old slowly began to look at this or that little girl. But that was only an exterior veil covering up what was growing within him.

More worthwhile were the daily visits next door. There, next to the town park, the municipal head gardener lived with his simple and efficient wife and two daughters, the oldest of whom, to Eberhard's sorrow, was very soon to die of typhus. The children's friendship began on the supposedly unclimbable wooden fence that separated the two properties. Soon Eberhard and both his younger sisters were running over there daily. He took the lead in the games. Once the high swing was a ship. "My ship plows through the waves, Fridolin! In the wind the sails swell out, Fridolin!" Another time the bean sticks from the gardener's house were fiery steeds upon which whites and Indians pursued each other. Yet a third time the heap of thick planks was a knight's castle from which it was necessary to kidnap the knight's daughter. How proud Eberhard was when he once sprained his elbow at this game. That was almost as good as the big bruise that came from a huge kick at football or the third accident he got from rowing, which was blood-poisoning: "Phlegmone manus," as he proudly called it. He can today still show the surgical cut made then. Through all this he neither shed tears nor uttered a sound! Only one of the doctors was mean. He had laughed loudly at the fifteen-year-old boy who, seriously concerned after being kicked in the lower abdomen at football, had asked him if it would be still possible for him to have children when he grew up or if that were impossible forever now.

A great deal in the head gardener's house was surprising to the Church official's children. How astonished they were when one evening quite unexpectedly the head gardener took off his boots and stockings. He let his wife bring in a huge foot bath and in front of all the older children calmly washed his feet. Things like that happened at home unseen. Eberhard and his brothers and sisters had never seen their father and mother except in quite correct dress. At the very most their father, absorbed in some learned problem, now and again had put on two ties one over the other when he got dressed and appeared like that at breakfast.

For a long time Eberhard was concerned with the question, which is better—this extreme and astonishing naturalness on the part of the gardener, or the apparently much superior respectability of his parents' professional dignity. At any rate the gardener's wife went much too far when she saw her twelve-year-old Susi give the fourteen-year-old Eberhard a childish kiss: she called out jokingly to him, "Look out, next year she won't do that any longer." That was enough to make anyone blush!

But they were all very warm and friendly at the gardener's house, and even if they never read the Bible, but only newspapers and technical magazines, even if they preferred to speak about apples and pears rather than about learned philosophical questions, they nevertheless gladly gave away the best fruit and lived peacefully together, which contrasted very favorably with the almost continually tense atmosphere in his parents' house opposite. What did that mean? Was social, Christian and educational superiority null and void? Eberhard could never get rid of this question.

It was the same at school. The best-dressed sons of officers and government members were continually shown up as the greatest scamps. Some of them had to be driven away from the grammar school in disgrace and shame. One of them had deeply hurt Eberhard after he had made one of his school books unusable. When Eberhard complained, he dared to offer him a nickel, as if Eberhard would allow himself to be paid for it! To be sure, for this affront Eberhard surprised him by twice giving him such a box on the ears that the other became as red as a crab. It was only through the authority of a school prefect that the two fighters could be separated.

Eberhard was sixteen years old now. During the summer vacation he went to one of his mother's cousins who had married a country parson. Aunt Elizabeth was very proud because she was not only the granddaughter of the famous scholar, Julius Müller, but also the daughter of a court preacher[4] to the Kaiser, whose significance politically and ecclesiastically appeared to her still more distinguished than her grandfather's learning.

Her husband, however, was to bring about the decision that was slowly being prepared in Eberhard and that would determine forever the direction of his life in an unheard-of way. Uncle Ernst had entered into the fight against the exploitation of the poor and their cottage industries in a Silesian weaving village with such courage that he had to be removed by the

[4] Rudolf Kögel (1829–1896).

ecclesiastical authorities and sent to another province. Not only the big industrialists, but also leading Churchmen felt themselves most unpleasantly attacked, "as if they had not cared enough for the poor in a Christian way!" This stand, which brought the weavers temporary help, already then captured Eberhard's heart for Uncle Ernst. And now with his older sister, he could spend four weeks with him!

Once more the parson had to go through some hard fights. The choir-master, who seemed extremely old to the children, had up to that time violated the girls of his top class. Now again the pastor turned with all his force to the authorities to protect the children, just as he had assisted the weavers in the mountains. The choir-master lost his post but the parson his congregation. The village lay too near to the big city; the moral popular feeling turned against the parson and stood on the side of the seducer of their own children.

Apart from the preacher's own family, only about four to eight people went to the church after that. The parsonage was barricaded like a fortress. The situation often seemed quite threatening. Soon, however, the opposition was satisfied by merely putting up a notice on a short-cut, a private road, "Prohibited for Dogs and Parsons." In the course of years the ringleaders disappeared for different reasons and finally, when the parson sprang into the village pond to save one of his bitterest enemies from certain drowning among the creeping water weed, the popular mood swung round. The church began slowly to fill up.

In that summer, when Eberhard stayed in a room next to his older sister as guest at the parsonage (that was in 1899), the waves of this village excitement were at their highest. That was something for Eberhard. How proud he was of his uncle, who preserved his cheerful quietness in the midst of every fight and with it all played "Robbers and Princesses" with the children. And then one night Eberhard's sister called out pitifully for help, "Eberhard, Eberhard, help! A man is in my room," and it seemed that the greatest opportunity for youthful heroism had come, probably never to be repeated. He was out of bed in a twinkling and appeared as he was in the quickly opened door, raised his unarmed hand, took his courage in both his hands, and roared out, "Get out, or I'll shoot!" Nothing moved. When the light was lit with trembling hands, there was nobody in the room. Door and window were shut from within. What had happened? At last his sister, lying in bed as white as a sheet, took hold of her left hand with her right and with some embarrassment explained the misunderstanding. "My hand went to sleep, so I thought it was somebody else's hand." So nothing came this time of the hoped-for heroism.

At breakfast they had a good laugh and their good-natured uncle said he had heard everything and straightaway thought the two had been dreaming. Eberhard, now that this adventure had turned out to be nothing, tried to compensate himself with the dog and cats, who enjoyed a good game. Of course his aunt was not satisfied; she did not understand the teenager at all. Not long before, their first child had been born for whom they had waited many years. How could a boy, who was otherwise so nice, be more interested in dogs and cats than in such a dear little baby in its sweet little basket! Only his uncle understood—Eberhard did not want even to study his vocabulary without the purring cat on his lap and the sleeping dog at his feet. He could make friends only with his uncle who had a living, joyful, and courageous Christianity, which the boy had never met before, and a love to Jesus and to the poor. Once when his uncle invited a man from the much despised Salvation Army to table and spoke with him as to a brother, listening with open-hearted admiration to the report of his salvation work, the uncle won the heart of the boy completely.

Previously Eberhard had kept an open volume of Karl May in his drawer while his school work lay on the table above. Now it was the New Testament that he wanted to hide from the curious gaze of those relatives who came in suddenly. The four Gospels had cast a spell over him. It was only his inner-most shyness that hindered him from speaking with his beloved uncle and asking him to help him find what he was earnestly seeking. It was only on his departure that he sought to be alone with him. "Oh dear!" he complained, "In our city there are certainly no people who can really tell me what Jesus is like." "Of course there are," replied his uncle, "You have only to look for them. Certainly there are some in your city." With a firm handshake, which meant a "yes" for Eberhard, they separated.

In his home town, Eberhard went first of all to board with a professor, a friend of the family. The old man and his son, in spite of their Zinzendorf Moravian piety, seemed to Eberhard to be too sober and pedantic, too exemplary and virtuous for him to be able to seek with them the longed-for inner help and encouragement. Alongside books on the primeval world, which brought him close to the great and mighty creation of the ice ages and prehistoric times, he read eagerly from the Gospels. One day he found in the desk in his room a copy of Thomas a Kempis's *The Imitation of Christ*. Now everything became clearer and clearer. Jesus became greater and greater. Discipleship of Jesus became more and more serious.

He was sixteen years old now. All the longing of his youthful blood began to be aroused in him. Bad comrades told him how easily and cheaply it was possible to satisfy all one's passions in the big city. The gloriously smooth marble statues of Venus in the city museum and the oil paintings in the art shops excited him so much that in the midst of his decisive religious struggle he went once more to that museum, as he said to himself, to take farewell from them for ever. Often he lay on the floor of his room in the house of the devout professor, his face pressed on the boards, his arms stretched out to fight through the hard battle that had broken out in him between the covetous love of Venus and the pure and infinite love of Jesus.

In this condition he returned in September to his parents, who had at last come back after several weeks' stay at the seaside. At first he withdrew as much as possible in his parents' house and went to the meetings of a young pastor, who then devoted all his joyful energy to young people.

Outwardly Eberhard's attitude to life had not yet changed. So it happened that on the 2nd of October, though he was walking up and down the main street with (in his opinion) his very nice ebony walking stick, yet his eye was turned inwards. Suddenly his reflection brought him to a firm resolve. He turned into the promenade. A quarter of an hour later he was in the study of the fair-haired young pastor. It seemed to Eberhard as though he had been expecting him for a long time. Amused, the pastor listened to Eberhard's first words, which appeared unaccountably to contain an attack on the pastor's addresses and Bible study. "Why do I hear so little from you about the Holy Spirit? I long for the working of the Spirit of Jesus Christ." "But my dear young friend," replied the pastor, "that is just such a working of the Holy Spirit that you have come now to speak with me." Eberhard had to agree, for when he was on the city's main street he could just as easily have turned off into an evil way! After a few more encouraging words from the young pastor, that in such decisive days he should not give up until he had found what he was seeking in his innermost heart, Eberhard returned hurriedly home.

As his room was too near to those of his brothers and sisters, he shut himself in the living room. At this time the living rooms to right and left were seldom used. From his small pocket Bible, which he had recently bought, he read aloud to himself the third chapter of John's Gospel. In the depths of these words, the picture of Jesus of all four Gospels, with all that was written in them, lit up for him. For again and again during recent weeks, he had read them all and absorbed them. Many decisive words of Jesus, especially the sharpest and most unrelenting, glowed in his heart, filling it from within with bright flames of light. How he loved this Jesus! How clearly he felt that the way of Jesus was the only possibility for true life.

But what was the use of all the words, heard and read, if this Jesus himself did not speak in his heart so as to give him complete, final and lasting certainty! But what did that cost? Already he had recognized that the social brilliance of an apparently privileged family was worthless. That would not be hard to surrender. It would be much more difficult to break off the little daily deceptions of ordinary school life. He had never seriously worked. At last he must make some progress out of duty to his parents and also now, for the sake of the honor he would owe to Jesus!

It would be still harder to retire from the role he had played among his school comrades. Here it meant denying himself. Because he had devoted too little industry to his schoolwork, he had tried by means of funny pranks to distinguish himself in front of his classmates right up to the present hour. This used to earn him many a punishment from the school. He now felt clearly that this childish vexing and teasing of the teachers was a contradiction to the love and respect he owed them as one who was about to become a Christian. His leading position in the small school club, his visits to horse races and the zoo, his loitering about on the street—this also sprang from the same stupid boyish ambition that now had to be crucified.

But hardest of all appeared to him to be the fight with his newly awakened senses, which made him long for beautiful girls. How would he be able to overcome such mighty powers? In this field, sin seemed to him to be the strongest of all, perhaps the more so as he knew his body had been kept pure and untouched. "O God, O Christ, I will not leave this room before you have accepted me and given me the strength of the new birth through your steadfast assurance." Suddenly, on the soft, deep, Smyrna carpet, surrounded by all the luxurious and superfluous furniture and pictures, the contrast between his life as it was and this inner fight in faith came most painfully to his consciousness. Only one thing could help in this fight, just as in the fight against his youthful ambition: the most outright public confession to Jesus Christ, the open declaration of war against all that was foreign and opposed to the way of

Jesus. The strength for this could only come through the for-giveness and removing of sin and its power, and through the new beginning of Jesus' life in the depths of his heart.

Now he grasped it. God gave his Son. He who believed in Him should live and receive divine life! So there came over Eberhard, who was still the same foolish half-grown youth, the stream of the love of God. It flowed over his heart as unspeakable joy. The finger of the Holy Spirit touched him. The voice of Jesus spoke to him, "I accept you. I come to you. Your sins are forgiven you. Go and witness to my truth."

With trembling heart and weeping with joy, filled to over-flowing with gratitude and urged inwardly to testify to Jesus, Eberhard got up. He did not know how long he had been in that room, overfilled with all kinds of valuables. He went at once to his mother and to all the others to tell them shortly what he had experienced and what kind of a turning point that meant. His mother only said to him, "You have always been a good boy." The others were silent. His father took up a rejecting attitude. Now a great fight began, in which Eberhard was to be joyfully victorious. There was such a very great love in him to all, yes to all, and he felt the certainty that love can fear nothing and has nothing to fear.

On New Year's Eve there came a pained astonishment from his family when Eberhard was asked to propose a toast as the punch was being drunk. He stood up and spoke of his meeting with Jesus and earnestly wished everyone that each might have the same good fortune to experience a new birth into a new life. It was quite clear that that was nothing for which anyone would empty his glass. As soon as this disturbance had been overcome and the New Year noise from the street had

been let in through the open window, Eberhard went quietly
to his silent room to renew his vow and to pray for his loved
ones.

Soon after, the conflicts became more serious when for inner
reasons he had to refuse invitations to children's parties given
by his parents' friends. The situation was the same later, when
as a young student he was invited to beer evenings at his
professors'. His father and mother laid great value on these
visits. In opposition to the wishes of his parents, Eberhard
rejected them completely. He would only go there when he
could quite openly point out to the hosts and their guests the
wrongness of their lives and challenge them in the name of
Jesus Christ to break away from all their surroundings. The
gentlemen who invited him did not want this. Eberhard's
father became extremely angry about such insolence from such
an immature young brat. The deepest alienation came between
father and son.

There were bad days when the parents themselves gave
parties, usually twice a year. At the time of the first collision,
Eberhard had dared to enter the learned sanctuary of his
father's study; in the large room Eberhard saw his father
standing erect before him as if he sensed some evil was coming.
For one moment Eberhard dropped his eyes to the clean,
waxed parquet floor. Then face to face—even if his heart
was trembling—he began his attack. "Father, I hear that the
food and drink for this party costs more than two hundred
marks. Those invited are almost all richer than we are. They
all have enough to eat at home. They will invite you again and
will offer you wine, roast meat, and ices, which are just as
costly. I know of poor innocent families in the east end of the

city, who have not enough money to provide their little children with sufficient milk. You know what Jesus said, 'When you give a feast, do not invite your acquaintances and friends, who in turn can invite you; but rather go out on the streets and invite the poorest people who cannot invite you.' You go to Church and hold morning prayers; but is this unjust life from God or from the Devil?"

This time the outburst of his father's wrath was indescribable. What an offensive brat, to be so impertinent and presumptuous towards his father, a father upon whom the highest Church authorities had heaped so many honors! Eberhard was locked up in his room for several days. There he read the Gospels. He was not so proud or so logical as to refuse to eat the remains of the party food, which were taken up to his room. The servant girls and the charwoman understood him best of all. He felt drawn more and more to the poor. He would have preferred to have put on the Salvation Army uniform so as to show outwardly too his turning away from the rich to the poorest society. It was his deepest concern to bring the joyful news of God's true freedom to the poor.

Yet he still went to the grammar school. He now concentrated on his books more than before. That autumn he had gone straightaway to each of his teachers at their homes to tell them about the inner change in his life and to beg their pardon for the way he had hurt and deceived them in his insolence by copying and by whispering to others. That was going to be quite different from then on.

Some of the teachers could not understand what had taken place. Slowly and after many setbacks Eberhard worked his

way upwards in the higher classes. At the beginning his comrades missed his joking and tomfoolery, in which he had taken
the lead before. They did not meet him any more at their
amusements. This did not please them. The worst elements
felt keenly attacked because of his sharp rejection of their un-
disciplined passions. But Eberhard, even if sometimes he moved
up to the third place, did not feel that he belonged to the
best boys of his class either, who were proud of their excellent
schoolwork, and of being at the top. He liked it when Professor
Winkler, who was rather a character, brought the top boy of
the class into the greatest perplexity, as for example when he
declared he would perjure himself if he had committed murder
so as to escape the death penalty!

Eberhard stood alone, but he did not have to remain so for
long. The young-people's pastor read the Gospels together with
him and with two other schoolboys who did not go to the
same grammar school as Eberhard. They began with Mark
because this Gospel was concise and confined itself to the
actual deeds performed by Jesus in His life. The other two
boys did not mean much to Eberhard. Yet this very small
circle gathered around the Bible, stimulated him to go beyond
the confession he had made publicly from the beginning and
go to work more militantly to win his schoolmates. At first
it was his two old club friends, Kurt Krone and Paul Schrenk,
who began to go this way of seeking God. Soon in the school
break about a dozen comrades gathered around Eberhard. In
the midst of the noisy playground, they stood under one of
the old chestnut trees in the quadrangle, or they strode up and
down seriously but joyfully in a long line. Eberhard spoke to

them of Jesus' decisiveness, of Him who demands everything
from us always and everywhere. Or he explained how great
was the joy and strength that went out from Jesus as soon as
anyone wanted to take Him seriously.

In the meantime Eberhard took over the leading of the Bible
study group, being then in the second highest grade at school,
because quite a number of boys from other schools were won
and because the cheerful young pastor left the city. Soon fifty
schoolboys from the higher and middle grades gathered together. Once more his schoolwork took a secondary place.
Some afternoons often five or six, or even ten or twelve, boys
climbed the wide comfortable staircase of the upper class
house to Eberhard's room. There he spoke with each one
individually. The boys confessed their small and greater errors
and told about their inner struggles against their hot young
blood. Nobody was judged. Yet the inexorable demands of
Jesus' pure life were disclosed just as uncurtailed as the strong
assurance of His forgiveness and living strength, which should
be strong in the very weakest.

Admittedly, there was a fanatical puritanism for a time
under the influence of Herr von Guertel, a peculiar East
Prussian nobleman, who lived in complete poverty in an un-
comfortable student apartment (whereas his grandfather had
driven through Königsberg with four white horses). This
threatened to twist the boys' souls by trying to deny anything
good in anyone else. Yet two other elements lived in the
majority of them, and especially in Eberhard. This was
quickly to put an end to such a deviation even if it did not
happen with everyone straightaway.

One was the social urge toward the poorest of the city, which often led Eberhard to the Salvation Army and to the slums. The other was the liberating love of nature, which just then had taken hold of the most lively members of the German youth. These were healthy and doubly weighty counterbalances to Herr von Guertel's intolerance. Nevertheless Eberhard and the other youths were never to forget that it was Herr von Guertel who deeply impressed upon them that the bright light of Jesus' life and His irrefutable demands were covered up, darkened, and weakened in most devout circles, whereas at other times (as for example in the Anabaptist movement during the Reformation period) the complete Christ without any kind of unhistorical weakening of His character dominated men's thinking.

From this time on, about the year 1901, Eberhard with the help of his learned father sought books that could bring the radical early Christianity of the Reformation baptizer circles closer to him. His father did not want in any way to encourage his inclination; but in some deeper talks he had to confirm that Johann Loserth, the investigator of Moravian Anabaptist history, was one of the most trustworthy scholars of today, and that he was quite right when he characterized those brothers as good, loyal and morally pure men with a rigorous love for Jesus. Eberhard's father only pointed out against this that in the course of history the Anabaptist Brotherhood had been almost completely exterminated by the Ecclesiastical and State authorities; world history is world judgment; so God had clearly not acknowledged them as the quiet Anabaptists had expected. In this manner they were disposed of. That did not convince Eberhard in the slightest. He replied at once that according to this way of thinking Jesus' death on the Cross could be used against Him. Without doubt that would be wrong. His father angrily cut short the talk and many years had to pass by before Eberhard achieved greater clarity in these things.

At any rate, for him neither his Christian youth circle nor the social and evangelizing work of the Salvation Army could be counted as a fulfillment of the early Christian ideal, which became known to him as a historical reality in the Anabaptist movement of the Hutterian Brothers in Moravia. Only in a very restricted sense did Eberhard succeed in interesting the other boys in these matters. For most of them it was enough to have the certainty that their sins were forgiven them and to feel God's love in their own hearts.

There was more in the Salvation Army. For there a deep social understanding for the outer and especially the inner need of the oppressed classes was added to the Methodist way of preaching conversion and salvation. The answer he once got from a certain Captain Twesten, who was hoarse from much speaking, made an unforgettable impression on him. Eberhard had made an involuntary remark as he saw a man who obviously had come down in the world, "What an awful face!" The Salvation Army officer said sharply, "What are you saying? What do you think you would look like if you had had to suffer what this unhappy wretch has had to suffer?"

That was true. That reply went with Eberhard throughout his whole life. He had things too easy. In spite of everything that is reported here he still did not manage in any kind of way to leave the privileged position in life he had received from birth. He went to the best school. He had a room to himself. He always had good food and the best clothes. It is true he neither drank nor smoked. He avoided the cafés and restaurants. He went neither to the theater nor to concerts. But he owned a sculling boat together with the comrades of the circle who followed him. In this they went on the river through the forests. He had time to go on rambles and explore all the hidden natural beauty of the surrounding countryside. He went swimming regularly, took up gym, played, and skated. He had a good time. Under these circumstances how easy was his Christianity when even as a tenth grader he spoke in public meetings in the town or in this or that village and was able to experience how at times many were moved to tears, perhaps even to revolutionary decisions. To be sure, in school it did become more serious. But what did his Christianity mean when all the outer security of his life remained the same, even though he did have to bear some unpleasantness for the sake of this joy-bringing activity, especially at home?

II THE STRUGGLE FOR THE WORD AND LIFE OF GOD

FROM THE ENGAGEMENT LETTERS OF EBERHARD ARNOLD AND EMMY VON HOLLANDER

GUIDE TO NAMES IN THE ENGAGEMENT LETTERS

Arnold, Clara
  Betty   Eberhard's sisters in order of age
  Hannah
  Hermann   Eberhard's older brother

Baehr, Else (Frau Oberstabsarzt) a friend who helped to bring about Emmy's conversion, in whose house Eberhard spoke

Brumby   town where the Freybe family lived

Freybe   name of pastor's family where Emmy lived as mother's helper or governess

Gerdtell, Ludwig von   evangelists in the revival movement
Kühn, Bernhard   supported by Eberhard

Hollander, von, Olga
  Else   Emmy's sisters in order of age
  Monika (Mimi)
  Heinz   Emmy's brother

Käthe   wife of Eberhard's brother Hermann

Ritzmann, Alwine   maid in the von Hollander family, converted through Emmy

Salzwedel   town where Emmy was trained to be a nurse by the Order of St. John

Sallwürk, von
Schulze   friends belonging to the believing
Sievert   circle in Halle
Stenzel

Still, Albert   friend of Eberhard

Voigt, Heinrich   Eberhard's "Uncle Heinrich," professor of Church history in Halle

II THE STRUGGLE FOR THE WORD
AND LIFE OF GOD
FROM THE ENGAGEMENT LETTERS OF
EBERHARD ARNOLD AND EMMY VON HOLLANDER

Introductory Remarks

Eberhard Arnold wanted very much to study medicine and become a doctor. His father did not allow it: Eberhard had to study theology. His father wanted him to become a pastor.

While he was a theology student, Eberhard was active as a public speaker in order to spread the message of the Gospel of Jesus Christ and to lead souls out of the Devil's bondage to faith in Jesus Christ and His work of redemption.

During the year 1907 Eberhard was studying in Halle on the Saale. In March 1907 Eberhard was preaching in the home of a believing woman, Frau Baehr. Here he met his future bride and sister in marriage, Emmy von Hollander, for the first time. At first sight Eberhard felt that this girl, whose name he did not know, was just as he had wished and had asked God that his future wife might be.

On Good Friday 1907 Eberhard Arnold went to J. Heinrich von Hollander, Emmy's father, to ask him for the hand of his daughter. He gave his consent to the engagement with the condition that Eberhard had to promise to pass his examination at the university and to keep the engagement a secret for the time being, since he would have to study for about two more years.

Eberhard and Emmy were engaged for over two and a half years. We have nine volumes of their letters, handwritten in German and typed in

English, which testify to inner struggles, to prayer and searching in the Gospels, because both were called and chosen by God to live a life of discipleship of Jesus.

The following section is made up of extracts from the first three volumes of these engagement letters. The poems have been translated simply for their content.

O Jesus, Savior

O Jesus, Savior, still far too little
Does my soul love Thee!
O Master, Lord, and King, lay now
Thy gentle yoke on me more firmly still!

Enkindle holy fire within me
To burn eternally and never cease;
For this there is no price too high.
Give me love that's limitless!

Let such fire be kindled in me
That nothing has power to quench it;
May I call none but Thee Master
And be Thine own in heart and soul!

To give myself to Thee completely
Is greatest joy and pleasure.
O take, O take my life completely!
Let fire burn within my breast!

My dearest Jesus, praise to Thee
For Thy Spirit's fiery power,
Which points the way to Cross and suffering,
Where God a new creation makes.

Whoever looks at the Cross must conquer,
For there everything is overcome.
There we cannot be defeated;
The power of sin is forced to yield.

The Lord has given His blood for me;
I may believe—I also went through death with Him.
O Hallelujah, I may live
For Him with every breath I take!

So shall this be true forever:
I myself no longer live, no—
My dearest Jesus lives in me,
And I am His in the radiance of the Cross.

August 17, 1906

In Thee, O Lord, Is My Strength!

In Thee, O Lord, is my strength!
In me, all strength I had is gone.
I see no help coming anywhere;
My thoughts turn to Thee alone.

All my longing goes to Thee, O Lord.
When all around me breaks and falls,
Thou dost hold me in Thine arms,
Yes, Thy love does not leave me.

In Thee, O Lord, is grace abounding;
On Thee I trust as on a rock.
Thou takest me ever forward, Jesus,
As long as my hand does not leave Thee!

July 30, 1905

[March 30, 1907]

Always Phil. 4:4! Eph. 1:14b!

My Emmy,

How poor is our speech when one is to convey such heights of splendor as I would like to do!

Yet how rich are our hearts that they can feel—no, more, *experience*—these splendors!

How wonderful it is, after all, that even in the most contrasting surroundings we can hold fast to this precious treasure in its fullness and enjoy it!

And how glorious it is that two people like us are able, in spite of the poorness of speech and in spite of all upsets and obstacles in place and surrounding, to share this rich splendor with one another completely and to enjoy and experience it with one another!

Among people in the jolting train, which contrasts so strongly with the last days, I am reflecting on the glorious grace God has poured on us—rejoicing in the invigorating memory of our unforgettable time together of complete, unclouded happiness, and in your sister Olga's little book, which is both so charming and moving.

Longing joyfully for you in Jesus, your Eberhard.

You will excuse the bad outward appearance which comes from the jolting of the train and my shortage of writing paper. But I couldn't help it, I had to write at least this to you. The rose is keeping marvelously. Greet everyone as warmly as you can!

Your Eberhard

Easter Sunday [March 31] 1907

Once again—Ephesians 1:14: His possession for the praise of
His glory!

My Emmy,

This morning the mailman had an unusual amount to do,
with the result that I was running back and forth from balcony
to window to front door for nearly an hour to see if he wasn't
coming at last.

Just then it suddenly occurred to me that I possibly had not
written or even told you my address at all! It gave me quite a
fright, because I thought of how awkward that would be for
you, and I was about to send you a telegram. But at last, at
last came the wished-for letter, and made me so very happy!

O Emmy, how *splendid* that you can write, "I do not want
to complain; we have much, much more to be thankful for!"
"I am too happy, too happy!" "United for ever in the Lord
our Savior."!

Oh, I wish I could hold fast forever to every word of those
marvelous hours on March 29 and 30!

But I was going to say, so *very* many things keep occurring
to me that we must talk over with each other, and in comparison to that the things we have already talked about are
only a very little bit. For I always want to tell you *everything*,
everything that I think and learn and experience.

You know, it is not without significance that God ordained
our betrothal on Good Friday. For our time of engagement
and our entire life must be lived completely under the sign of
the Cross, the Cross that has brought us with God into the
glorious relationship of children of God; that has obliterated

our sins and revealed the highest love of our God and our Jesus; and that has for us the power of having died to sin and the world, so as to live for Him!

And your Christian understanding will grow in proportion as the joyful determination of your will to serve Him alone increases. Pray in all questions, simple, childlike, and trusting, and He will give you His answer ever more clearly. And then, study your Bible with eagerness and devotion. What do you think, shall we both read the same each day, a chapter at a time maybe? Would you rather a Gospel, or a Letter? Then we can always be speaking and writing about that. What would you think of Matthew? Or what is your suggestion?

I am so *very* glad that you too love so much to see *Jesus* always in the center. That alone is healthy Christianity. Not teaching, but *Jesus*; not feelings, but *Jesus*; not effort, but *Jesus*! Always, nothing but His will, His peace, and His power!

And on a wonderful walk during which Papa [Arnold] had me tell him about you the whole time, he told me something that made me very, very happy—that he too sees our engagement as given by God. About your family, too, he wanted me to tell so much that what I know about them so far was much too little. He rejoiced very much about our happiness, and gave me some important things to think about. Chiefly, he confirmed that I must work with all my energy toward being able to give you and myself a secure living as soon as possible. True, I do not draw from this the same conclusion that he does, that on this account I must aim for a position with retirement privileges, such as a parish, for I know that my Lord will best take care of me and mine if I joyfully go His way as I recognize it, even if this may seem outwardly disadvantageous. And this is exactly what you think, my Emmy. Please write to me about this too!

Above all, see that Jesus occupies the first place every moment and place everything under Him, in particular our wonderful relationship. Test everything, pray about everything, and tell me everything!

I am yours, you are mine, and *we are His*!

Your happy Ebbo

Halle, April 1, 1907

My Eberhard,

There again you have had a fine thought, that both of us want always to be reading the same in the Bible. Then I can always ask you about everything. I think I would rather read a Gospel first, and Matthew would suit me very well, or John. Write which one you would rather. I still wanted to ask you something about the Lord's Supper. Gerdtell[1] says it is merely a meal of fellowship and remembrance; of forgiveness of sins nothing is said in the Bible, he claims. Why then does it say: 1 Cor. 11:27–29, and in Jesus' words of instituting the Lord's Supper it says "forgiveness of sins." Please write how you feel it.

About your position, whether you should become a minister or a missionary or something like that, I cannot advise you either. I can only say, "Where thou goest, there will I also go; where thou stayest, there will I stay; thy people are my people; *thy God* is *my God*. Where thou diest, there will I also die, and there will I be buried!"

Your Emmy

[1] Evangelist, friend and contemporary of Eberhard, leader of revival movement.

Easter Monday, 1907 [April 1]

My Emmy,

Oh, if only I could sit here with Emmy now and talk with her about our wonderful happiness, about our great Jesus and the total dedication to Him!

Please write to me exactly about whatever in my articles you

1) have read with especial enjoyment and blessing;

2) have not understood well;

3) have not found right.

You can imagine how enormously eager I am to hear this.

But I would also seek contact with the more simple of God's children; the fellowship in Christ knows no class distinctions— here we are all together one in Christ (Gal. 3:28).

Now good night, it is half-past nine!

Ebbo

Breslau, midnight April 4–5, 1907

My Emmy,

Pastor Paul has been in Christiania [Oslo], and told us now about the wonderful revival movement there in which many, many have made a complete surrender to Jesus, and the Spirit has come down with a power as at Pentecost in the Acts of the Apostles; thus people there today speak in strange tongues and what they say is in part clearly understandable to those who know these languages, and, without the knowledge of the speakers, it was a clear proclamation of the Gospel, always with the demand of full dedication. O Emmy, I kept thinking, if only you were here and hearing how quietly, soberly, and yet marvelously the Spirit of God works in our days! Let us trust in our God for great things, in prayer on the basis of His Word, and He will do great things!

Your happy bridegroom

Breslau, April 6, 1907

My Emmy,

Not the feeling, but the *will*, makes the character, including, and especially, the Christian character. Often we must go quite soberly on the simple way of strict obedience, and at other times the Lord overwhelms us with floods of happiness and joy. The peace of God is not a feeling. It is more; it is a relationship of the soul to God, the fact that the reborn is a child of God.

I believe that in the baptism in Matthew 3 it is the first time in the life of Jesus that His role as representative comes quite visibly to the fore. He became man in order to redeem men as representative saver and sufferer. As a member of humanity, and as such bearing the sin of humanity—not His own—He allowed Himself to be submerged for the forgiveness of sins in order to fulfill all righteousness.

Endlessly happy through Jesus and you,

Your faithful Ebbo

Breslau, April 7, 1907

My Emmy,

I have finished reading *The Court Preacher*, was very deeply moved, and could hardly part with it. You know, Emmy, the close of it drove me deep into prayer that God may keep you for me my whole life long so that we may come to the Lord *together*, experience His appearance in the best way, and *together* go to meet Him, our highly praised One!

Your faithful Ebbo

Breslau, April 8, 1907

My Emmy,

Matthew 5:13–16 is also of special significance to me. Just as the sources of our life are hidden from public view (6:1–18), so must its fruits be clear and striking in words and deeds (5:13–16, etc.). According to my understanding, 5:39–41 means that for Jesus' sake we want to bear everything in love and patience, and do even more, not insisting egotistically on our own rights—always in order to conquer the souls through love.

Your faithful Eberhard

Breslau, April 9, 1907

Beloved Emmy,

Verses 1–6 [Matthew 7] are important guideposts for dealing with souls, for which we are made capable only by the way described in vv. 7–14. Verse 12 sums up briefly our attitude to them. Isn't that ingenious how it all connects together? The Sermon on the Mount is directed first to the *disciples*, but then to the larger group of *people* as well (ch. 5:1; 7:28, 29).

Your Eberhard

Breslau, April 10, 1907

My Emmy,

O how I look forward to seeing you the day after tomorrow and to being able to discuss everything with you! I hope very much to find you really well and recovered. I will confess to you, I had to think that you are going to be very much disappointed in me in many ways when you get to know me better, even though I show myself to you just as I am, as well as I am able—of course. But then I went on my knees again and couldn't do anything but always thank and thank! I was and am quite *indescribably happy* that through God's incomprehensible grace we are indissolubly bound for ever. I don't believe you have any idea yet what it means to me. Only eternity will show that.

For your very loving, full letter I thank you a thousand times! Like yesterday's, it came very early and brought me the deepest joy. Of course I can't know why you feel you said too much, but Emmy, I consider it very good that you expressed plainly your view on the question of social life, and so forth. I agree joyfully with you point for point. "Put off the world, and put Christ on; this way the thing is fully done," says an old verse.

The answering of prayer depends on two conditions:

1) *Faith*, that is, the previous certainty of being heard in the dedication to Christ (compare condition 2) e.g. Matthew 21: 21, 22; Matt. 17:20; James 1:5. As a true Christian—and this is all we are talking about (2)—I *can* believe and be certain *only* when I am sure through Word and Spirit that my prayer is in accordance with God's will, for example for wisdom

(James 1:5), for grace (Romans 5:2), or for the Holy Spirit (Luke 11:13), and still other things.

2) The second condition is called in the Bible "in the name of Jesus," that is, in His place, on His behalf, in His purpose and Spirit, as if He himself were doing it! For example John 14:12, 13; John 16:23. This can of course be done only by one totally converted to Jesus, one who through Him is righteous and renewed (as in James 5:15), one in whom Jesus lives and rules.

You see that such senseless prayers as asking that I should go through my last two years of study and get my degree of Doctor of Philosophy in one week, or receive 100,000 marks— and objections to this type of prayer are very numerous—are entirely outside of the Biblical way of thinking. Certainly, we may and we should ask for earthly things as well, but always in the name and the Spirit of Jesus Christ and in faith in Him and His Word, and abandoning our self-will. We simply must *have made a complete commitment,* surrendering ourselves fully to Jesus, if we want to understand and experience the Bible.

In Matthew 7:7–11, not every request is meant (it also says there, *Seek! Knock!*), but depending on the context, which one must always take into consideration, it means: 1) for the Holy Spirit for right judgment and concern for souls (Matt. 7:1–16 and Luke 11:13) and 2) for entry into God's Kingdom, conversion to Jesus (seeking and knocking [in the context of Matt. 7] verses 13 and 14).

Now I have got quite carried away by this great subject,

after I had intended to write only a little to you today because by Saturday I have such a *terrific* lot of work to do. *Pray very much for that!*

Verses 15–23 [of Matt. 7] say quite clearly that not prayers, and not great deeds in Christianity either, give release from condemnation, but solely the complete, absolute submission of will to God to do His will consistently (verse 21) in faith in Jesus, based on His Word (v. 24), thus to the obedience of faith.

Essler is a *very* consecrated man of God. Remarkable that one such as he should be not a bit prepossessing outwardly.

Fräulein von Nostiz lives at Ludwig Wucherer Strasse 37, probably on the third floor now with Fräulein von Haeseler (also a truly converted and dedicated lady).[2] I would be glad to get the Siewerts's address from you, since I am to be staying with them. My sister Betty could not come along, since she is still with the dentist and is prevented by other things. She is trying this way and that. She is looking forward very much to Whitsun. Loving you daily more in Jesus,

Your faithful Ebbo

Breslau, April 11, 1907

My Emmy,

I woke up very early today and went joyfully out on my bicycle into the fresh morning air. When I returned, your letter

[2] Fräulein von Nostiz and Fräulein von Haeseler belonged to the same revivalist circle as Eberhard and Emmy.

was already there, and again it gladdened and strengthened me so indescribably!

The parable of the unjust householder is very deep and important.

John 6:54, I believe, just like verses 35, 47, 48, 51, uses this image to show clearly that we *receive Jesus within us* completely, who was *crucified* for us, as our Redeemer for eternal life! This *dwelling of Jesus in us* is the great life mystery; it is what chapter 6 is all about. The Lord's Supper is the tangible realization of this glorious fact for believers.

Your faithful Ebbo

Breslau, April 12, 1907

My Emmy,

How happily I thanked the Lord again and again today for your letter! For what you tell about is *pure grace*.

I am *very* fond of Fräulein von Nostiz, just because of her openhearted, joyful way of not hesitating to say everything that is just then moving her. She is an especially blessed disciple of Jesus. I think her way of sometimes coming out with things too deep or difficult for the others to understand comes from thoughtlessness and is thus a weakness. To fellow disciples like you or me, however, she can only do a service by it, since we reach out to have Jesus ever more fully and to penetrate more deeply into His glory and that of His Kingdom. It was surely from the Lord that she and all of you had such a talk with your parents. Their statement about being too old is proof to me that they were deeply impressed.

You are right: we want to confess to all believers as our brothers and sisters and to place their conduct in the right light, with the peace of Jesus. Go your way, Jesus' way, with all the greater love and all the clearer resolve! We *must* be persecuted and suffer for Jesus' sake (Matt. 10:22, 34–39; 2 Tim. 3:12). This is a necessity of nature and our joy (Matt. 5:10–12; 1 Peter 4:14; James 1:2! and other places).

Dear Emmy, we have it too easy rather than too hard. I always am doubtful about the real existence of Christianity in a person if he does not suffer for Jesus' sake. We must on no account create persecution and antagonism for ourselves— that would be sin—but neither must we omit *one* word or *one* action which we ought to do for Jesus, for fear of it. The more we confess Him, the deeper will our peace become, for Matt. 10:32.

Full of joy,

Your Ebbo

Lichtenrade near Berlin,
April 21, 1907

My Emmy,

In my uncle's[3] study, where I have fled so as to have some quiet, I think of you, that the Lord may make you perfectly happy, right now and always!

O Emmy, what glorious days those were in Halle, when I was able to see you so often. Yes, the Lord alone has led us together! To Him be eternal praise and glory for that! No

[3] Eberhard's uncle, Ernst Ferdinand Klein.

human being, no power, can part us, for always and every-where we are one! Hallelujah!

How much I would like to know now what you have been doing and experiencing. Perpetually, at the station, in the meeting, in the church, at meals, in the garden, everywhere, I have thought of you and prayed for you. I have not received anything from you yet and I suspect that the uncertainty of my address is at fault there. On Monday evening I will be at home again.

Your Ebbo

Lichtenrade nr. Berlin
April 22, 1907

Dear Emmy,

Your so very loving letter of the 20th gave me infinite joy and refreshment. I walked up and down in the garden and discussed each point with Jesus, and I was so happy and firm in faith while doing this!

Yes, Emmy, Matthew 18:19–20 fits so well to the two of us. We have become united to pray that Jesus may accept each of us and us two together completely, completely as His possession at His disposal; that we may know Him more deeply and allow Him to work on us; and that we may gain many souls for Him. Oh, we have become united about many things, including prayer for my studies and exam, and for your God-willed activity.

Well, Emmy, I must be off to Salem now. You too have a guardian angel whom God has sent out to serve you. Matt. 18:10; Heb. 1:14! They are not little children with tiny wings, the way church art represents them, but according to Scripture they are MIGHTY *spiritual creations of God!*

Happy through you,

Your Eberhard

Breslau, April 23, 1907

My Emmy,

I am so especially happy that the Lord is increasing your love for souls, so that through you too very, very many may be saved! When I think that for the next two years I will hardly be able at all to be at the disposal of human hearts, a thought that is very heavy for me, it is really a marvelous comfort and a very deep joy for me that you, my Emmy, are to be used by Him all the more in this time. Clearly, I will pray for this heartily and joyfully. You know, Emmy, often it seems to me as if we were not separated at all, so fully do I feel our unclouded community and unity. Yet neither one ceases to be an individuality, for each one wishes this very thing for the other, that his Christian character really stand forth, distinctive and independent. Thus love gives release from the ego and thus at the same time it strengthens the God-willed individuality.

I always pray for you,

Your Ebbo

Breslau, April 28, 1907

My Emmy,

Today there is such a tremendous lot that moves me that I don't know how I'll ever end this letter.

Just think, this morning at 8 I went out on my bike because

I had no peace at home waiting for your letter. There came the mail carrier past the bridge. I was off my bicycle and asked him for letters, and he gave me—printed matter! Quite crushed, I then rode out into the wonderful morning air! To right and left the young green was sprouting, and the sun was shining, so warm and friendly. And I kept silently praying, "Lord, make me joyful in spite of it, even if I have no letter! And bless, bless my Emmy, and let me *thank* Thee that she has so much to do for Thee that she cannot write!" Oh, it was so glorious outdoors. Along a little stream with beautiful woods and bushes and a pleasant view across the fields I got off, read Matthew 26, and prayed for you and myself. About 10 o'clock I was back home again. You can imagine how infinitely happy I was when two letters were there with your beloved handwriting! Warm thanks for everything you wrote! Your parents too wrote so very lovingly.

I am so unspeakably thankful to you that you help me in all these things and will help me more and more to go the straight, narrow way of Jesus, no matter what it costs!

Because of this I also had to thank Jesus that you and Else[4] have stated decisively that under all circumstances you will do God's will, which you recognize in the Word. Without this resolute stand there is no rebirth. That you are placed so seriously before the question of baptism moves me very much. I have prayed urgently for you that *God*, and no one else, shall lead you.

Then I right away looked up my old notes, looked through them for you, and wrote to Else besides—which is also meant

[4] Else (1885–1932) Emmy's sister and most faithful co-worker and co-fighter of Eberhard and Emmy; see pp. 211–227 of this volume.

for you. This matter is closely connected with the question of the outward form of the true Church (*Gemeinde*) of God, about which we want some time to talk together directly.

I am so terribly happy that you, God willing, will be with me in three weeks.

If you follow my request on the next page, we will just be reading John 3 together on Whitsunday! Because of my work in the first place and because of you in the second place, I have the great wish that the day after tomorrow we start on Mark; we would already finish it on May 16 and then take John. As you can see from the enclosed schedule, I am now reviewing the Gospels, that is, comparing and learning the three synoptic Gospels until May 16 and then John, all in Greek of course. In the morning I read only for my heart, and then I work it through. For you too I think it will be good if you first read the Gospels thoroughly (I would also compare Luke) and then take the Acts of the Apostles and the Letters. Please write to me right away if you are in agreement. The Gospel of Mark presents to our eyes the acting and working of Jesus, more than His words, in an uncommonly vivid way.

Then there were some things to prepare at the university, and I did not always possess the *strength for work* that I wished for myself. The last days were the best. Joyfully forward now! Let us *believe* and *pray* more, and more seriously, and I will achieve more and more from week to week! Oh, how I need your intercession and help! This week, then, the enclosed schedule holds good completely.

The fact that he [Charles Finney], our dear Fräulein von Nostiz, and many other people of God, and above all, the

apostles on the day of Pentecost, received the Holy Spirit
with powerful stirring of feeling and outward signs must not
cause us to think that the Spirit is limited to such accompanying phenomena. That is far from being the case. No one can
call Jesus *Lord* (thus belonging to Him) except through the
Holy Spirit (1 Cor. 12:3; Rom. 8:9, *14*).

Those whom the Spirit of God guides and leads, they are
God's children. For the most part this comes about quite
naturally and unnoticed, through the Word, sober reflection,
and circumstances. Thus, for example, our engagement was
without doubt a leading of the Holy Spirit. When we know
Jesus, love Jesus, follow Jesus, we have the Holy Spirit, for
He shows and glorifies Jesus! *John* 15:26; 16:13, 14. Therefore, for all these reasons you, my Emmy, without doubt have
the Holy Spirit through God's grace.

Now it is important, however, to distinguish here. The same
Spirit who (1) *makes His dwelling* thus in each one who is
converted and glorifies *Jesus,* wants (2) to *take possession* of
him and *fill* him so fully and utterly that he will be at His
constant disposal as His *instrument for people.* This means
being equipped with the Holy Spirit *to serve;* this was what
gave Finney the strength to save so many thousands; through
this we have today such powerful awakening.

The Spirit, then, wants (2) to *convince the world through
us* of sin, justice (saving, making just), and judgment! John
16:7–11.

Of this mighty service we are capable ONLY through the
Spirit. In the great, God-willed sphere, only if we are *filled*
with the Spirit. The more Spirit we have, the more souls we
will rescue. We will always be able to receive Him, who is a

person, whenever we are dedicated in faith to Jesus. Yes, we *have* Him. Sometimes we become full of Spirit suddenly, but also sometimes gradually, with every service more and more, if we allow ourselves to be detached more from our self and trust more in Him alone, totally. Let us pray, pray for the Holy Spirit. Please read the chapter in both the Torreys about this! Go on asking if anything is still unclear to you! This matter too is *simple*, quite simple. But it appears difficult to us. I too was moved by it for a long time without becoming clear about it.

I pray especially for Olga [Emmy's eldest sister]. I believe she lacks full trust in Jesus. It seems to me she is afraid it could go badly if she obeys Jesus *completely* and belongs to Him *completely. This is no faith* in the full sense, thus it is none whatever. It is a seeking and a tentative trying out.

Your Eberhard

Breslau, May 5, 1907

My Emmy,   *Jesus is Victor!*

I have found *very* often that I was sharply rebuked when God gave me strength to do His will, also in this very work of saving for Him. I will tell you much more about this—to His honor. You know I find it hard to speak about this. But to you I will tell everything, what is most heartwarming and what is saddest, and you will receive and understand it all *in Jesus.* For the work in God's Kingdom there is hardly anything more important than to be deaf to praise and blame by fellow-men. For this shows up whether one has died to oneself and

lives for Him alone, for Him alone! Certainly we want to
learn from everything, but to be dependent on or directed by
nothing *except Jesus*. Because of this human weakness—which
is in many of God's children as well—and because of the
danger of self-admiration, one very soon comes to the point
of speaking as little as possible about the ways one has been
used by Jesus, out of grace.

O Emmy, what grace—let us tell each other this over and
over—that God has brought us together! Now let us make
use of it and be strong, so that we don't overlook or conceal
the weaknesses of the other out of a wrong kind of love, but
rather listen to each other with the *divine* love that originates
from Him, and strengthen each other mightily in the holy
fight against world, Satan, sin, and self, which we both have
to carry on. This is the bond we have formed! And Jesus is
Victor! Hallelujah!

All your struggles, Emmy, I have felt with you very much.
I am acquainted with them from my own very painful experience. But Jesus has always remained Victor, and will reveal
His victory more and more! I pray constantly with joyfulness
for our *parents* and all our brothers and sisters. Olga worries
me very much.

We want and are able to be ever joyful and full of peace
when we suffer for Jesus' sake, but in thinking of the others
we must be sad. Matthew 5:11–12; John 16:33; Matthew
18:7; John 3:16. We *love* the others most purely in the sense
of John 3:16 when we *hate* them, altogether in the sense of
Luke 14:26. Hating means here, as in many other places,
"putting up a fight against." What is meant is *not a feeling*,
but *taking a stand*. If we have taken a stand for Jesus, we

cannot do otherwise than to put up a fight against our un-reborn parents and others, since they are not able to judge anything by what is divine but only by what is human. This *strengthens* love instead of weakening it. Above all we must take this stand against our *own life*. Luke 14:26. Thus we are urged to pray that they may be rescued and that we may in no way give offense wrongly, but always remain *in Jesus*.

Let us ask Jesus and always pray in all things, e.g. about how long and how often we may write to each other. Not what *we* want must guide us, but *only* what Jesus wants.

Remaining always yours,

Eberhard

Breslau, May 9, 1907

My Emmy,

Your letters have *moved me deeply*. May THE LORD guide you! And He will do it. I am so *very* happy that *He* is leading you more and more to recognize His will, so that you *independently* take up the same determined attitude that I want to take.

This is the best way for us to support each other and make each other strong. The Lord will also constantly make us *equal* in all understanding, for He has led us together into *One*.

I can't go into the questions further today, however *very* much I would like to. But I *pray* unceasingly for all.

Everybody, and that means Else and Mimi,[5] alone and *in*

---

[5] Mimi stands for Monika, Emmy's younger sister, who later married Georg Barth.

independent clarity, must act in a resolute and consistent way on the *irrevocably clearly* recognized will of God.

for
Else { Romans 14:23b!
too!   1 Cor. 10:13!
       1 Cor. 15:57, 58!

Greet everyone, especially Else.
Loving you in the determined obedience to Jesus Christ,

Your faithful Eberhard

Breslau, May 11, 1907

My Emmy,

I am so very thankful for your dear letters because they let me experience everything and consider everything in prayer with you so completely, everything that all of you are encountering.

I am writing you already today instead of tomorrow for two reasons: first and foremost, because of what you have indicated about the matter of Pastor Hobbing[6] versus Frau Baehr. This strengthens me in my opinion of Hobbing, which is *much sharper* than I wanted to tell you at that time and than you should give Olga any inkling of without having proof in your hand.

Dear Emmy, we are concerned with our friend and sister in Jesus, the honor of our Lord, as well as the relationship of trust between His disciples! *Here there can be no postponement!* The matter must *immediately* be *absolutely cleared up*, what-

[6] Lutheran pastor, close friend of Mother von Hollander and Olga.

ever it may be. First Corinthians 13:6 applies here—the truth
—and above all *Matthew 18:15–17*! (It *doesn't* say sins
against you but simply *sins*!)

Someone has sinned. Consequently it is first, Olga's; second,
Else's and your and Mimi's; and third, my duty to clear up
the matter with relentless straightforwardness. *Olga* must talk
the matter over clearly with Frau Baehr, or else she is not
submitting to the word of Jesus and is therefore included in
Matthew 7:24–27, especially verse 21. If Olga does not do
this, if she does not clear an accusation against a Christian
woman, then *you* others are obliged to demand that she tell
the plain truth, and to lead the way yourselves. If you do not
find the way, *I* shall take the matter in hand very energetically,
and this would be less pleasant.

So, my beloved Emmy, I think my point of view is clear.
By means of this way of obedience (Matthew 18), I have often
attained tremendous things to the praise of Jesus and to the
disgrace of the enemy. No compromise is possible there.

By the way, my Emmy, it is an old story that disciples
living in God's blessing and in the strength of the Spirit are
constantly slandered; for example, Matthew 5:11. Disgusting
lies have been disseminated about Gerdtell, and also about
von Viebahn, Modersohn, Girkon,[7] and others. About me—I
am telling you this for you alone—people have claimed that
I stole from my parents' safe, and other absurdities as well.
My uncle, Pastor Klein, had eighteen or nineteen lawsuits and
disciplinary measures undertaken against him in one year, because of his witness against sin; in these cases the lies were in

[7] Three outstanding men in the revival movement.

part supported by perjury. Jesus vindicated him *wonderfully*.

In this matter too, be just as calm as you are resolute and thorough. Let us *pray*!

The second reason I am writing you already today is that tomorrow after 7 o'clock I have a White Cross[8] talk to give to perhaps a hundred young people of fourteen to eighteen years old, which is supposed to show them the way to the Savior. Please pray *specifically* that some may clearly be rescued, reborn! We have promises.

I am so very glad, Emmy, that you are developing one-sidedly in the right sense. We live ONLY for Jesus; we read, speak, and do *only* things that are FOR HIM, and *nothing* else, not even what is noblest. Oh HOW RICH our life becomes through this poverty! 2 Cor. 8:9. John 15:16; 10:11.

So let us, Emmy, be joyful, unaffected, innocent, natural, and unforced in our determination. This is very important; otherwise we will fall under pressure of the law which is not the Spirit of Jesus, the Spirit of Jesus being a Spirit of freedom, that is, of the *voluntary, joyful obedience in the strength of faith*. (Letters to the Romans and Galatians.) So never allow yourself to be controlled by moods and depressions sent by the Enemy; instead look to Jesus (Heb. 12:2) and go your way quietly, *ignoring* Satan, for he is overcome.

I am glad Mimi is taking it very seriously. That is what she must do, or else she will not be able to withstand the struggles of the coming months. For it is going to be very serious.

But over and over again 2 Cor. 2:14, with regard to everybody and everything!

Baptism is *very* serious for me, and I have *never* considered

[8] Movement for moral purity.

it as a secondary matter. It is only that my recognition until now was a different one. In my leaflets I tried to present the nature and significance of nominal Christianity and its limitation through infant baptism.

This, then, is my stand until now. Let us *review* it together, my dear bride. We are of course both prepared to obey Jesus, however He gives His word.

Oh, what a lot we have to talk about! It is high time that you come. What has happened with Frau Major Köhler?

Christ was active already before His incarnation; 1 Cor. 10:4, 9; John 1:1–4. Some few Old Testament believers like Enoch lived in fellowship with God (more about him it does *not* say), certainly through the Spirit of the death of Christ operating in advance. For otherwise they would have had no forgiveness. Jesus Christ, *yesterday* and *today* and the same *into eternity*. But everything face to face! May the Lord let us grow in *grace* and *understanding*.

Always one with you into eternity,

Your Eberhard

Breslau, May 13, 1907

My Emmy,

Warm thanks for your loving, detailed letter! I am so sorry and I feel with you very much in having to go through such a lot. But it is good, Emmy, that we are in the midst of the fire; and struggle is a sign of life. We want to persevere in joyful faith! Not one millimeter shall we turn aside from the clearly recognized way of Jesus. And should we be forced through obedience to Him to bring on further conflicts, then we *can* do nothing else but go His way, without a single concession to the right or to the left. It is so marvelous that we are at one in this, and I *know*, Emmy, and *knew*, that you are ready to do *everything*.

But in point of fact the way is difficult in this case. However, my Emmy, I still maintain that something *has* to happen. I have prayed over it and reflected on it, a great deal in fact. I think Mama [von Hollander] must *either* take back her statements, that is, allow herself to be persuaded to think better of it, *or* let us know what caused her to make these statements. I fear it will be difficult for you to attain that. Or maybe you will? I also believe that for me to give a firm witness for Frau Baehr (who by the way takes a very decided stand on this very point) is the right thing. I therefore submit to you my outline, with the request that you evaluate it and send it back by return mail. Pray about it!

About Olga I will not write anything. I would be glad of an opportunity to write to her again. I am praying very earnestly for her.

About Pastor Hobbing too I am saying nothing today. I have already prayed a great deal for him, alone and with others, in Halle of course, and am praying for him now. I am very sorry for him.

My mother has been wanting all the time to write to you, but she has had a great deal to do. Today she is going to write, and I believe to Mama [von Hollander] as well. There was a huge tea party here today. I soon fled to my room and then went to the YMCA, where God gave victory in answer to our prayer. Quite a number—I don't know how many—confessed their sin, personally and in the meeting afterwards, and handed themselves over fully and "singlemindedly" to their Jesus. To close with, one after the other praised and glorified our glorious Savior. Must we not go on our knees again to give thanks that God, on the prayer of His weak children, does miracles again and again? Yes, our whole life a song of praise! Hallelujah!

This week, besides my studies, I also have to write an article I promised to do for the *Alliance News*.[9] Yesterday I did not manage to do any work, although I believe we are not slavishly bound to the law of the Sabbath, but stand above it.

Please greet everyone very much!

May the Lord be close to you with His peace that surpasses all thinking. I thank your brother and sisters very much for their greeting. Saturday evening, how splendid that will be! I thank our Lord over and over again out of the depth of my heart that our relationship to each other is so marvelous.

Your Eberhard

Halle, May 14, 1907

My Ebbo,

Your letter made me *very* happy this morning. Your letter to Mama, too, is very good. Only don't mention Pastor Hobbing; that wouldn't do any good, only harm. We want to pray for him very much, especially for Olga. She always

[9] Magazine of the Alliance movement, which tried to unite the revivalist groups that had stayed within the established Churches with those who had left them.

emphasizes that Jesus must occupy first place, but otherwise everything is allowed. She always weakens it so much. I think I talked things over with her too much, as at first I regarded her as belonging completely to us, and she now uses this by talking about it with people who have no understanding for it whatever. For example, she (as well as my parents) has talked with Henny Zabler and her mother about the baptism question. They of course consider this sheer madness. This doesn't surprise me; I would have been just the same earlier on. I am sure Olga does not reflect in the least that she does terrible harm to the cause. For Olga says, for example, that Else *can't* have herself baptized. If we should happen to go to Dorpat,[10] she would surely be sent to Siberia because she belongs to a sect, and they are considered politically dangerous there. I told her I see it from a completely different point of view; I believe that God will lead everything marvelously. This makes her angry, and she says I don't want to understand her. But Ebbo, don't write to Olga anything of what you would perhaps like to say to her; that would *not* help *at all. Only* through love can we win Olga, and only Jesus can do this through us.

I am very glad and will thank God for having blessed Sunday evening so richly. I prayed for that very much too. I am very happy,

Your Emmy

[10] University city in Latvia, belonging to Russia, of which Emmy's father was a graduate.

Breslau, May 15, 1907

My Emmy,

I wouldn't have thought that the fight would become almost as hot with you as with us. It was wonderful that before all these scenes took place God had led us in our talks to the subject of the persecutions of His followers, and that even twice! It is wonderful; even the very noblest cannot stay neutral and friendly—in fact, he is the very one who can't. We must *decide*: *for* or *against* Christ! *With* those who belong to Him or *against* them! Anything else is a wretched whitewashing of decay and death. Anyone who makes the pitiful attempt to go along with both sides plays the saddest part and finds himself in nothing but impossible situations. Yes, let us pray, pray, that God will open all their eyes! I am doing it faithfully!

With us in Breslau, dear Emmy, you will find an *outwardly* quiet situation. But the powder keg could blow up again fearfully at the next spark. The most extensive liberties are granted to me after God has given me victory in the bitterest struggles. I trust He will give it more and more purely each time. There are great differences between victory and victory. The unconverted members of my family have become *more and more deeply unhappy* in the years since my conversion; it often tears at my heart. Outwardly their circumstances are very *prosperous; outwardly*, toward the world, they seem quite happy, but inwardly there is terrible strife and unpeace. The children of God in our family ought to take a more decisive stand. Then, only then, will the others do so. At least that is how it seems to me. About *all* this I will tell you a great deal.

How shall we ever get through all that we have to say to each other? I don't believe we ever shall.

It will already be clear to you that you have a great task from the Lord for my family, for all of them, but especially for Clara and Hannah both of whom are looking forward very much to your fellowship. I expect from the Lord that your joyful, loving nature and your unaffected, resolute witness will win hearts utterly for Jesus. For this we must pray humbly and earnestly, for we do know, and we want to grasp it deeply, deeply, that ONLY HE can give it. And He *wants* it.

In great love,
Your Ebbo

Halle, May 16, 1907

My Ebbo,

This morning your letter and the one to Mama arrived. I look forward very much to you and your family and have a *great* deal to tell you. You know, I am quite confused by everything and keep having to raise myself up by Jesus. In my view, Else is not acting quite rightly and honestly toward our parents. I shall tell her this today, for she can do the whole cause a lot of harm. Our parents have yielded to Else to this extent, that she is to wait one year with her baptism, and then if she still wants it, she will get permission for it. To be sure, during this time she is not allowed to meet with any "Rebaptizers" or the like. She is allowed to go to the meetings, and to Frau Doktor Schulze too, since they have no concern whatever with such questions. Primarily, Frau Baehr and Fräulein von Nostiz are

STRICTLY forbidden to her. Else does not go to them anymore, but she does meet Frau Baehr at Frau Doktor Schulze's house and has secret meetings, even secret correspondence, which she receives in the vocational school. She also says that from June 9 on she will certainly have herself baptized.

Now today Mama told me she had lost all trust in Else, for she hinted to me, even asked me directly, about these "secret little meetings." I just don't know what attitude I should take to it. Else says she has to meet with Christians, that it is her *support*. She is quite right about this, but as I see it she has not acted openly, and after all, the meetings are still allowed her. Above all she has her Bible, and I would think it more right if she showed she had fully enough in Jesus, even if for a time she cannot go to her dearest acquaintances or friends (Mama has been saying all the time it is just that she is crazy about Frau Baehr); or she should say right out that she is meeting with them anyway, but she doesn't do that either. What do you think about this, my Ebbo? Do still write that to me. I am unable to feel it is right, and it will harm Jesus very much. I am not going to help Else either, and shall talk very seriously with her afterwards as soon as I get her alone.

Incidentally, Father wants to write to you today about Frau Baehr. Please DON'T answer until I am with you. We *must* talk everything over first. I still have a great deal to tell you. Father at first did not want to let me go on the train; he thought I should not be allowed to arrive later than eight o'clock. Yet now he is allowing it after all. We want to pray very much for my stay in Breslau. I will come, then, just as you suggest. I still want to write to our dear mother. Her card yesterday made me *very* glad. Everyone greets you very warmly.

In faithful love in Jesus,

Your Emmy

Breslau, May 17, 1907

My Emmy,

I was very deeply distressed by your letter and would perhaps have done too much, my danger being to act too impetuously. Now I am joyful and full of trust in Jesus. My Emmy, I am fully of your opinion, down to every detail, and hope to God that your talk with our dear Else will be led to the goal, that is, to the recognition, confession, and giving up of sin.

Oh, if she *could* come with you! But I have not been able to attain that. Greet her warmly! She must become *quiet*, completely quiet in the Lord; otherwise she has no promise. The Spirit of Jesus is called peace, not unrest!

I want in any event to give you a time of joyful refreshment and rest, and for this I pray very much. In the course of the days we shall talk everything over thoroughly.

Your bridegroom

After the Farewell

No, I could never be joyful
If Jesus were not my Star.
Only in Him are we blissful,
However far away!

Before Jesus I am quiet,
My King fights for me!
—It was His gracious will—
He bears us mightily!

O Jesus, trusting in Thee
Is complete happiness!
Whoever believes will joyfully see
The Savior's light!

The more I give myself
To Thee, to be Thine own,
The more purely shall I live
To the glory of Thy Name.

To Thee we give our pledges.
We vow to Thee alone!
Through every hour of time
Thine eternally!

E.A. May 29, 1907

Halle, May 30, 1907

My Ebbo,

At last I am managing to write you and thank you for your letter, the flowers, and the poem. You know, I can only raise myself up by our Savior. Oh what wonderful, blessed days those were when we could be so completely together. How wonderfully we understood each other in all things; in prayer we were so united.

Else is relatively well. She has to stay completely in bed. Our parents are furious about the baptism and want to make every effort to prevent Else from going ahead with it. In other things, however, they are very helpful to us. They were also somewhat angry with me because of the letter to Else. They considered it crazy. From time to time there are great upsets.

Please do send me some of the photographs that Clara took of us.

Your poem made me *endlessly* happy.

Your bride

Struggle and Victory

The desperate battle rages all around
Against Satan's mighty columns.
Then we must rise to watch and pray!
The victory will soon be won!

A General leads us, Jesus Christ,
Who never lost a battle.
The weakest fighter is victorious
Since He has won the victory.

The world with all its force and guile
Would rob us of our courage.
But look to Jesus Christ alone,
Although the world spews fire.

Fear and anxiety have left us
In spite of afflictions beyond measure!
As long as you cling close to Christ,
He will never leave you.

He calls to us: Be comforted!
I have conquered the world
That rages furiously around you—
Defeated through my suff'ring.

So courage! Here is total victory
At the foot of Christ's Cross!
For He who mounted the Cross for us
Has mastered Satan's pride!

Only one thing—you must taste this same death
Right to its bitter dregs!
You know He lives, your Lord and God.
His life will comfort you!

He will give you His divine strength
To conquer as He does.
The Lord in you will work the miracle
Of one victory after another!

E.A. May 30, 1907

To Emmy

But yet I know only one way
On which it is certain
That you are always near me—
That way is Jesus Christ.

Yes, Emmy, turn your face to Him,
To Jesus Christ alone!
For there where our beloved Master is
My eyes are ever turned!

E.A. May 31, 1907

Halle, June 1, 1907

My Ebbo,

It is already three days since we saw each other! I would like to tell you everything, to experience everything with you, and to pray with you. But I know you always do this for me, just as I do for you. It was so wonderful that we were able always to say everything to the Lord together.

Just now Hannah[11] left. I was very sad. She settled in very nicely with us and formed a friendship especially with Else and Mimi; they want to write to each other too.

We sang a great deal out of the *Reichslieder*, and evenings we read and prayed together. Of course I always prayed for you. The day before yesterday we read, on Hannah's request, Isaiah 40, and yesterday John 17. Yesterday afternoon Olga, Mimi, Hannah, and I went boating on the River Saale.

Today there is a great excitement at home. A "Rebaptizer," Fräulein Händler, gave me a bunch of lilies of the valley this morning, which had a note tied to it with one of the "Daily Texts";[12] I only discovered this after I had passed the little posy on to Else. Olga, who was present, told Mama about this, and so there was again a great upset because I had again let in the "brothers and sisters in Christ." She said these "familiar relationships" were terrible to her. Mama wants to write to you that you should forbid me to go to Frau Baehr. As soon as I am forbidden to do this by my parents I will of course not do it any more; so far they have not done that. Therefore I will probably go there again today.

---

[11] Eberhard's youngest sister.
[12] From the *Daily Texts of the Moravian Brethren.*

Now I still wanted to tell you about Else's talk with Doktor Witthauer. When she came in Doktor Witthauer greeted her with the words, "But you have another new hairdo; you look like a poor penitent." (Else now wears her hair with a simple center parting, which Mama actually likes very much.) When Else replied that this was not so, Mama told him that Else was run-down nervously, that she had heard the Gerdtell lectures. After that a certain movement had formed here, to which a Frau Oberstabsarzt Baehr also belonged, and Else had also joined this movement. Doktor Witthauer said that even a healthy body could not withstand inner struggles, much less a sick one. When Else said that she had peace, he said he already knew this expression from Frau Baehr (about whom he said to Mama another time that she wasn't quite right in the head). He said *he* was religious too; he had a sensible religion, without extremes, but just always staying in the good middle of the road. He had had enough of Frau Baehr; one time when he had treated her sister-in-law during an illness, Professor von Mehring as well as he had said she had religious delusions, but Frau Baehr would not hear of it.

Today or tomorrow I will write to Lisa Franke about the Bible House in Freienwald. May the Lord lead everything according to His will! The same with Stettin. Mama is going to speak to Doktor Witthauer about my health.

I have not yet read the *News* of the German S.C.M.[13] or the other writings. I haven't got around to it yet. Many thanks for them. . . .

[13] German Student Christian Movement

But now I must close. Please pray very much for me, for Stettin and everything. Greet your dear parents and Betty very much. I love them all very much.

In Jesus,

Your Emmy

Breslau, June 1, 1907

My Emmy,

This time it is so *very* much harder for me to be separated from you. I am properly ashamed that I simply can't succeed in being really joyful. But it is spineless, and it grieves the Lord if we give way to that. We want to be brave and trust in Jesus! Feelings must not rule us, but only the Lord and His will! The more we subordinate our wishes to His will, which wants *only* the *best*, the happier we will be!

> Send us the strength, fill us with power,
> To conquer over the Enemy!
> The strength that all our grief allays
> And comforts every weeping heart!

I am enclosing two more poems for you, which I made for you in these days!

I am writing to you already today because I have so terribly much on my heart!

Does Else have peace in Jesus? Is it her will to yield to authority, as it is surely right to do, and to hold out for those weeks in bed? I am worried about her restless zeal. How will June go by?

Can you express to Else in loving quietness, after praying

in common, our doubts about her concept of baptism, without giving the impression that you want to persuade her at all costs? Or have you already done all this, and what is Else's stand on it?

The most important thing for me is that by letter we tell and ask each other everything, just as we did during those glorious days in Breslau, so that I can be certain you are not experiencing outwardly or inwardly anything either wonderful or difficult that I do not know about and for which I do not pray. I will keep it so. You will see how soon you will write ever faster with nimble pen when you continue to give me news so faithfully.

Your Ebbo

Comfort and Joy!

This joyfulness makes us quiet:
In Him is all our trust.
The way His will leads us
Is for us both the best!

So we are always joyful!
We are never far apart.
We know we are so blissful
In Him, our faithful Lord!

Our happiness is complete
For we belong together.
In joy as well as sorrow,
I am yours and you are mine.

E.A. June 2, 1907

Breslau, June 2, 1907

My Emmy,

The enclosed verses are meant to give you a share in my joy in the Lord and in you. I am now quite peaceful again and happy in the will of my Lord.

At the moment very serious thoughts are occupying me. Brother Frost, about whom I have already told you and written you many things, was with me and has given me a lot to think about. First of all he strengthened me in thinking that the Word of God is sufficient for us and that all books and teachings beyond that are to be rejected. It was also very important and a great joy to me that for him too, consecration consists in obedience to Scripture and that his inner attitude is summed up in the one word, "Jesus!"

On the other hand I consider it wrong that he rejects all books except the Bible and will not read them. There are after all—thanks to God—many books written for the purpose of understanding the Bible. Should we not use them to penetrate ever deeper into the Word? What I do want to learn from this is only that the word in books must *never* be made to supplant the Word!

What causes me more difficulty is his principle about obedience to parents. He says rightly that we should obey them in everything insofar as this can be done in community with Jesus. Now he said that, as a high school and university student, I had done much too much work for others (to help them inwardly), and as a consequence I probably had not followed the wish of my parents to accomplish a great deal in my school work and studies.

I want to consider this reproach very carefully. It was said completely in the love of Christ. Only I believe that whereas my dear father either forbade or disliked any attendance at meetings, any work for souls whatever, the Bible and the Spirit surely demand the opposite. It is hard to see clearly the line of demarcation here. Pray that I may recognize what is right! It is similar with our later calling. To what extent is the will of the parents decisive? We want to be very careful to act here completely in the Word of Jesus.

For the time being I am drawing the practical consequences by pushing on with my studies with all the concentration God gives me strength for, and catching up with all I have neglected. *You must pray very much for this!!* I too want to keep on always writing to you about what I am working on: next week only the New Testament and a sermon critique, if I stick to my intentions.

Yet I believe I can never regret having worked with souls for Jesus, and I must hold to the fact that it was His service and His Spirit that urged me to it, even though much was weak and wrong and only a small part of the results is enduring.

O Emmy, help me and let the Lord give you deep insight into my corners and weaknesses that hinder the working of His Spirit so that I can be used in utter purity by Him for eternal fruits, without sham success and without harmful side effects! In word and work, in all our being, may Jesus and *nothing* else be seen! I believe I need a deeper purification from self, to be more completely filled by the Holy Spirit. For this we want to pray for both of us! The condition is the obedience of faith. And this we want to achieve in Jesus!

In Him I pray for you as

Your Ebbo

Halle, June 3, 1907

My only Ebbo,

This morning I received your dear letters and poems. You can imagine how happy I was. Your poems moved me very much, quite particularly the last one. *That* is just how I think. That hour a week ago today was a very holy one. Beforehand I told the Lord everything that concerns me. I prayed very much for you and our families, very especially for Betty too. Greet her very warmly from me.

I too have the impression that Else's illness is minimal and should be taken mainly as an opportunity to quiet her nerves. Yet I still have the worry about her lungs, for something must be the matter there.

I talked very seriously with Else today about baptism, her restlessness, etc. She wants to reflect on everything again in prayer, especially the point of waiting until May 1908. In any case I told her that I regard it as totally wrong if she should slip out in some unguarded moment and have herself baptized, and she agreed with me.

My parents are very inconsistent about their permission for meetings and fellowship with children of God. One time they allow me to do everything, another time they forbid everything. They keep Mimi away from everything (except for Pastors Vonhof and Hobbing).

About what Brother Frost said to you, I am reflecting a lot and will also pray about it. I think too that we have enough in the Bible. Still, we can also enjoy books that are written to honor God. I think that is definite.

What he says about the other, one can understand from a certain point of view. However, I believe we can be very thankful to God that He has used you for His service so early already, and we must not regret that. For our later calling we want always to pray a great deal. Then God will surely show us what is right.

In Jesus we want to be completely one in prayer.

Your faithful Emmy

Please greet your dear parents very much!

Halle, June 3, 1907
10 o'clock in the evening

My Ebbo,

Your letter of this afternoon moves me deeply and sends me very much into prayer. We want to ask God over and over again to show us His way so clearly that we know for sure: *this is His way.* Then we will go that way and not worry about people, even if it is our parents. Perhaps God will show us a way that our parents want as well.

Yes, Ebbo, you are right; let us request of God clear insight to recognize our faults mutually and to help each other with them. O Ebbo, tell me everything and help me to put aside my sins through Jesus so that I become completely pure through Him. Also pray very much for more Holy Spirit for me, to be newly filled with His Spirit. You know that I probably have the Holy Spirit, but that I believe He does not yet possess me;

and you pray for this too. For Jesus did promise that where two of us unite to ask for something, He will give it to us. We want *always* to pray for *everything* together. I always pray for you, that God may fill you ever more and more with His Spirit. I thank Him for having given me so inexpressibly much grace in giving you to me; I thank Him that I can always tell you everything and that you will always help me to become more like Jesus. That is really infinite grace from Him; I can never give thanks enough for it. I also pray a lot for your studies, that God may give you health and strength. Always write to me what you plan to do and what I should pray for especially.

Your faithful Emmy

Halle, June 5, 1907

My Ebbo,

My godchild Hermann [Freybe] is 2½ years old now, and his sister Renata is 10 months old.

I also believe that my parents hope the Freybes will soften my Christianity. But my Savior will protect me from that. On the contrary, I ask God that I may become ever firmer, more solidly based, and ever holier through Jesus, and that He may release me more and more from my own self. Insofar as I know the Freybes, I definitely believe that they only rejoice about decided Christianity and will never seek to weaken me. If they do, I'll tell them right away very definitely the first time. May God show me His will!

Your bride

My Ebbo,

I spent a few hours with Frau Baehr yesterday afternoon. On Sunday I shall go again, and pray very much beforehand. Yet I would *prefer* (but as God wills; I only seem to myself so terribly unworthy) in the time I am here to remain quiet, so that I myself can get further, and so that God can still disclose to me many things I must still get rid of so as to be able to give myself completely into death. I always think there *must* still be something or many things in me that hinder the Spirit of God. Then I have often reproached myself for not telling of my experiences when for example I was trying to rescue a soul, but instead told of others (e.g. about you) and made these experiences facts because I believe them but I myself have not (not yet) experienced them.

It was said yesterday in the Alliance class (to which I was able to go, with difficulty, in the evening) that one did not need to experience everything, but that we are *allowed* to take everything in faith; only *then* would personal experience come. What do you think, my Ebbo? These things cause me to think a great deal and also bring me to prayer. You must also pray *very* much for me that I may come to clarity. It is surely the Devil who makes me afraid. I always have to think, 1 Peter 5:8, "Your enemy the Devil, like a roaring lion, prowls round looking for someone to devour. *Stand up to him, firm in faith,* and remember that your brother Christians are going through the same kinds of suffering." And, "You *were* straying like sheep, but *now* you *have turned* towards the Shepherd and

Guardian of your souls." (1 Peter 2:25, NEB) These and other words give me strength again, and also Isaiah 43:1 and 4. I find Ezekiel 3:17–19 *very serious.*

I also say to myself over and over again, "I can do nothing at all, and Jesus can do everything; the smaller I am, the more Jesus can do in me."

Praying for you,

Your Emmy

Breslau, June 9, 1907

Jesus!

My Emmy,

I am so extremely, indescribably thankful and shall praise Jesus for it my whole life long and into eternity, that you draw me upwards so!

Because of this all your letters are so infinitely valuable to me that next to my Bible I regard them as my greatest treasure. It occurred to me today that through the very fact of being separated we have after all the greatest blessing of having our letters from this glorious time for ever, expressing as they do so completely, insofar as that is possible, our thinking and feeling.

But at last I must be more down-to-earth; I want to write you many things that I am full of. I will begin with what is most important to me—that is you—then proceed to the others, and will close with myself.

I am so happy that you write, "The less I am, the more

Jesus can do in me. I nothing, He everything!" and that you repeatedly express your complete trust in Him!

The other point I have laid very much before the Lord— that you fear there is something in you that particularly hinders the Spirit. You know, I believe you should let yourself be freed from gloomy brooding of any kind. If such a mood comes to you in which you are downcast and feel your sins and your incapacity to serve, yes, in which perhaps the Enemy tries to sow doubt in your heart about whether you are saved, then, Emmy, go to Jesus as you are, as a poor, weak human child, and *praise* Him, *honor* Him, *thank* Him for obtaining full salvation for the most wretched so that *we* need do *nothing*, *He* gives us everything. Ask Him for forgiveness for having grieved Him by mistrust as if He demanded more than open- ness, and thank Him that this forgiveness is *yours* because you are redeemed by His death. Then ask Him to show you relentlessly everything that is evil about yourself, and tell Him firmly that you want to give it up immediately. Then reflect quietly and do what you must do, in joyful confidence in Him, *having* forgiveness and grace even *before* you have *carried out* everything, *being fully determined to do so*. If the Lord cannot show you anything, all the more reason to be really joyful! By this He means, "Rejoice in my grace! I know you love me, and I am in you. In my time, the right time, I shall show you everything to lead you onward." Then continue on your way full of joy and thanks!

Be joyful! Realize that if you are not, you are disgracing Jesus. Don't we all have cause always to be joyful? Yes, rejoice always! Then one thing more: Some of your questions were

already clear to you from the little book for the awakened!
We don't want to let ourselves be robbed of what the Lord has
given us, but instead to use it for ever more glorious fruit.

Trust in the Lord also in regard to the Holy Spirit! Believe
His words that He gives Him to you. He gives Him to you
just as you need Him. If what He has in mind for you is
quietness, the Spirit will give you insights into yourself and
Jesus, and will not give you strength to evangelize and save
many. If He leads you to one soul, He will then give you just
enough strength to enable you to witness to Him in weakness.
In doing so He will not at the same time also give you the
grace, while on the way there, to lead this and that one to
Jesus. It is not we who determine our service, but the Spirit,
and this He does in the most natural way. In God's eyes the
smallest, quietest service or obedience is worth just as much
as the mightiest deed of faith. In fact, the latter does not
always stand as high as the former.

So let us become still, my Emmy, go our way in joy, pray
earnestly for His Spirit, trust Him in every service, and thus
glorify Jesus by our peace!

Thus I pray for you and know that the Lord will answer
me and make you a witness who will praise and glorify Him
with her whole life!

You see then that it must surely be the Devil who gives you
unrest? John *15:11*; *16:33*; *14:26, 27*; 11:40; 10:27, 28, 11;
8:36; 5:24; 4:14; 1:12, 16.

You will then also see clearly that you certainly have a
right to witness to the truth even if your experiences are not
quite of the greatest. For our guide is the Word, not our
experiences. John 17:17.

Please do write to me what particular points you have in mind there. It always seems to me that you have enough of Jesus to be able to witness to that. And you have after all broken with relying on feelings! Faith stands on the WORD, and thereby on the *Cross* and *resurrection*. The Rock is outside of us, not in us! Psalm 40:2–4, *3.* To be sure, then the Lord is also in us.

Does Mimi perhaps adapt herself too much to circumstances? To Pastor Vonhof she should go very often. That is very fine. About Pastor Hobbing I don't want to say anything. But certainly she ought to win for herself by faithful, determined asking and fighting the possibility of having fellowship at least now and then with the other children of God, our friends. We want to let Mimi act quite independently, in accordance with *her* conscience. But you must speak with her about it some time.

Betty was asked recently at a party whether my strict Christianity was not causing a rift between her brothers and sisters. (The world does *not* consider her one of us!) She says, "Not in the least! One doesn't need to talk about those topics!!" This really nice answer, friendly to us, I consider unchristian. I said to her, "But I would like so much to talk with you about it, and I would like to do it very soon" (something like that). At that she laughed, again very friendly and poised, not liking what I said.

Recently I gave a definite witness before Papa, Mama, and Betty that I consider as Christians only those who live entirely for Jesus and that in the true Church (*Gemeinde*) there are but few Christians. On another occasion I told Mama and Betty that the reason I would like so much to be in the

Salvation Army was that I would then not be honored by the world. Betty didn't understand me at all. Mama even said that was really quite a menial attitude. True, good people should be recognized. Something of that sort.

Recently we had a wonderful Bible class about waiting for Jesus.

I trust in Him fully, for the future as well. He will lead us surely and clearly, and make His way sunbright for us! About Frost's scruples I am again quite at peace. I have told my parents that I could have worked harder and that I am very sorry about it. But the work for the Lord was, I am convinced, a task for Him, and a wonderful task, for which I praise Him!

Full of joyfulness I pray for you,

Your bridegroom

Halle, June 10, 1907

Jesus!

My Ebbo,

Your long letter moved me and made me very glad, and the same with the poem.

I am very glad you were able to do so much work in the last week. Thanks to the Lord for this! May He give you ever more power and keep you well to serve Him! I began the Letter to the Romans on Friday. It is rather hard to understand. Especially hard for me to understand is chapter 3, the first half. I know we once discussed this passage in connection with the baptism question.

The witness you were able to give about Jesus to that student is really splendid! It is certainly wonderful how God leads. If only this student would decide completely for Jesus!

I believe I now know my great fault, which I constantly commit. I am concerned too much with myself, with my sinful nature, instead of with Jesus. "My eyes are ever on the Lord, who alone can free my feet from the net" (Ps. 25:15, NEB). That is how it should be. I have done what you wrote to me. I have asked Jesus to show me everything that I need to let go of or that prevents me from being filled with His Spirit, and I have promised to give it up as a sacrifice for Him. One of the things is that in my prayers I have often promised Him more than I have kept to.

Now I have asked Him in my prayers only to guide me by His Spirit. I will tell you an example. You know that we promised Him to give up everything, your and my honor, and to acknowledge *only* His honor. *And that is how it has to be.* But you know, that is sometimes really hard, especially when you are praised! I already felt this at that time, and I was not honest about it to God. I wanted to be, certainly, but did not believe that I was doing that, and only from faith does the strength to conquer come. You know, I find it hard to write this kind of thing to you, but I am doing it anyway because after all we want to help each other to blessedness and you are to pray for me, and besides, I think it is right to tell you everything so that you don't overestimate me. Should the Lord show me still more, I shall write that to you too.

Then there is something else that bothers me. Recently we discussed Col. 3, "We have died and risen with Jesus, and have done away with everything; then we are reborn." It is not so with me. Since my conversion I am recognizing only *bit by bit* all the sin that is in my heart (not all at once). Am I then converted, but perhaps not yet reborn? Of course I am determined to give up everything that does not come from Jesus. Such thoughts often come to me. Am I reborn? But I am looking at myself again and not to Jesus, and that is already wrong. Jesus says, "Whoever believes in me will not see death forever." I do believe; am I reborn, then? I also *want* to live my life completely according to Jesus' Spirit and purpose and for Him.

I shall be very glad when I have written everything to you now so that you can pray for me. I also need much, very much, from Jesus, and much praying from you, and I know you do that.

Praying for you constantly,

Your faithful Emmy

Breslau, June 12, 1907

Psalm 126:4! Be exuberant with joy! Matt. 5:12. Luke 6:23. Phil. 4:4.

My bride,

Your letters are becoming ever deeper and richer in content, and give so much to thank for and to pray for. Your 50th letter in particular gave me so much blessing. But I am equally happy and even more joyful about the happy beginning of the second fifty letters! On Sunday I shall, if God wills it, write to you in detail about everything.

Yes, you are right, Emmy, that is the main point: look only

to Jesus! Heb. 12:2! He who has given our life of faith also completes it, as the Crucified and the Exalted! You will see in my poems the same struggle—often in rather strong expressions (1905)—how an oppressive awareness of sin is totally conquered through looking toward the Cross. You will read with me tomorrow Luke 7:47. Thus even sin will make *Jesus* greater and more glorious for us if only we look away from it, to Him! As in verse 50, "You shall go in peace!" Not in reproaches of conscience. That is done away with.

Emmy, you *are* reborn, for you have the life from God, for you have *Jesus*. (You love the Word, the brothers, etc.) You must never let the Devil take that away from you. He who is converted is reborn. In Col. 3:3 our new life in faith and resolute obedience is gloriously (!) dead with Him, living in God. That is my and your life, Emmy. But read on, what the Apostle writes to the *same* people in verses 5–11! How much of sin and of the old nature must still be put aside before Christ is all in everybody! Renewal is not yet completion; the rebirth is only the beginning of purification. It is the normal thing for us to recognize more and more what is bad in us, so as to put it aside completely through Christ and thus to move always forward. Please look once more into the booklet for the newly awakened if it is not clear to you yet!

The second thing, too, I have experienced myself and thought it over a great deal. I think it is alright for me to rejoice when you are praised, because I love you and because I want Jesus to be glorified through you. Look, if something good is said about me, you need only say or think (if the good is really true): "I praise Jesus for blessing him. May He go on doing this more and more fully and completely! He has it from Jesus." Should the person concerned be the one we love most of all, then we should rejoice all the more that he too experiences the glory of Jesus and helps to glorify Him. This, more than everybody and everything, is how I unite *total love for Jesus* with *total love for you,* joy in Jesus with joy in you! Can you keep it this way with me too? Oh, THAT WE BOTH MIGHT GLORIFY HIM!!

Very happy in these thoughts,

Your Ebbo

Halle, June 11, 1907

My Ebbo,

This morning I awakened very happy with my Jesus, thinking of your verse,

Whoever looks at the Cross *must* conquer,

For there everything is overcome.

There we cannot be defeated;

Sin and delusion yield and fall.

When Jesus comes, then Satan must retreat! Then after I read with joy Luke 5 and had prayed for you and myself and all our family, especially for Hannah, I was very happy, and gave myself over anew to my God. This is more or less what I wrote to Hannah:

1) Actually it is natural for us to witness to that which is our life—Jesus! 2 Cor. 5:15. 2) Whether there are people who are not held to the world by even a single thread? We *are* bound indissolubly firmly to Jesus. We must let go of everything that is not Jesus. But He says, *Matthew 19:29:* what He gives we may accept, and thank Him; *God gives beyond*

our asking and understanding. I found this out *before* I was at all clear that I would have to let many things go for His sake. 3) Whether every vanity, love, etc., is such a thread? *Yes.* We may, however, bring everything to Jesus, and sacrifice to Him what He wants. We may and should love, also someone in a quite special way. Jesus also loves John and Lazarus more than others. We should and can also love the world, even our enemies, and this in such a way that we want what is best for them—to rescue them! That is about what it was, only in much more detail. Dear little Hannah!

Praying for you constantly,

Your bride

Halle, June 13, 1907

My Ebbo,

Today Papa is writing to you. He expresses himself very harshly again and again about the "Rebaptizers' Society." He believes it is linked with certain human ideas and will not let himself be persuaded otherwise. He knows that you and I have a different attitude, that we confess to them as to brothers and sisters; still it won't harm at all if you express this once more. Perhaps you can on some occasion express that you will never join a religious party with human goals and aims, but only where nothing but "Jesus" is preached. This is actually what he thinks about you too. I believe someone must have persuaded him that the Baptists are trying to attain some political goal and are drawing as many as possible to them by religious inducements. That too is the kind of point on which one can never come to agreement with him, as I have often told you.

Because of this we don't want to defend the baptizers in general (he no longer attacks individual ones), but we want *only* Jesus. You confess only to Him too; that we hold to the brothers and sisters, he can see anyway. And Ebbo, Papa has trust in you; you must not take that away from him!

Otherwise everything here is quiet and peaceful at the moment. We read and pray together. Mama even prays and reads together with Else. This came about as follows: recently she said to Else quite touchily, "You always read with friends, but never with me." Else immediately answered, "That's really splendid that you want to read with us; let's do it right away." They didn't get to it that same day. But the next morning Else called Mama, saying she had promised to read with her. It was something very embarrassing for Mama; still she did it, and Else thanked Jesus afterwards that she was able to read in the Bible with dear, dear Mama. Mama was quite touched! Now Else comes every morning and reads and prays with her. I find it glorious! And it all came about in such a matter-of-fact way. You know, I would find it hardest of all with Mama. But Else gets along very well with her.

This afternoon Pastor Meinhof is to hold a lecture here about 1) infant baptism, 2) baptism of believers, 3) rebaptism. Perhaps I shall go and listen. In any case I want to go to the Alliance meeting today.

Your faithful Emmy

Halle, June 14, 1907

My Ebbo,

Yesterday's lecture by Pastor Meinhof about baptism is attracting general attention! I myself was not there. But today I already heard about it from three quite different sides. Pastor Meinhof spoke *very* much for infant baptism, and a great discussion followed. His lecture had the result that Herr Franke decided *only* after the lecture to have himself baptized, and a daughter of Professor Blass told Herr von Sallwürk today that she also is now beginning to wonder.

But I must close now, for it is nearly 11 o'clock.

Praying for you,
Your faithful Emmy

Halle, June 15, 1907

My Ebbo,

After Else and I were in a Bible class at Frau Doktor Schulze's, where we were together with a number of children of God, I am sitting down to write to you. We spoke about Romans 1. We want in general to go through the Letter to the Romans, and this is very welcome to me as I find it rather difficult.

But imagine, I am after all rather depressed today. I found it tremendously difficult and didn't succeed at all in being very friendly to Frau Baehr, although today she was friendly. Thus I think that I have not died with Christ after all, or else I would not be able to feel the least bitterness toward anyone, especially toward a child of God who stands so very much above me. I am very sad about it and ask Jesus to become completely master over me. I really don't want to be anything in human eyes, and maybe it is just good if even children of God do not understand our actions, so that one becomes still more free from all human beings. I mean the matter of baptism.

The freer we are from men, the more firmly we are bound to Jesus, who always understands us with our weaknesses.

Your faithful Emmy

Victory in Spite of All!

To my Emmy

Sin seizes hold of our weak hearts,
Temptation nears us everywhere!
Satan stirs up the bitter pain:
Is life but fall on fall?

From dreary darkened depths arises
The fearful questioning of doubt:
Is new life sown here
Where sins live on and on?

O soul, what is it that He said?
Are *you* this new life that He means?
What man would not be in despair
If this was to be the way his soul is purified.

No, *Jesus* is the Bread of Life!
O hallelujah—*He*—thy life!
Not thy death, but His on the Cross
Shall raise thy heart up to His heights.

Look up! With joyful eyes of faith,
Look to Jesus alone!
We shall never more look backward;
We have built on Jesus only.

Within us, all is hollow and wicked;
Only His strength is noble, great.
He whom Jesus frees is truly free,
Is strong in Him, and empty of himself.

E.A. June 16, 1907

Breslau, June 16, 1907

My Emmy,

You do me the greatest loving service by being completely healthy and completely joyful!

This brings me to the deeper point that I think you brood too much and look much too much into yourself. Today's poem will tell you what I mean. You must hold *much more firmly still* to the first section—that nothing but looking to Jesus gives deliverance and certainty. Clearly, Emmy, we surely want to and must put up a very determined fight against every sinful impulse, and we cannot do this seriously enough, but we must not remain downcast. If we have discovered something evil or if we have fallen in any way, then we go IMMEDIATELY TO JESUS! And what happens when we come to Jesus and turn our backs to sin, the old or the *just* committed (it's all the same)? We are not thrust out, but are drawn to His heart *as His own* and filled with *forgiveness, strength,* and *joy,* so that we rise again with praise and thanks! Rom. 5:1,2. We *have* peace through faith (read Olga's pamphlet); we *have* access to grace! Hallelujah! I just want to write down a few passages about joy from the Letter to the Romans:

15:13. God fill you with pure joy and peace!

15:6. That you may praise God with one mind, with *one* mouth!

15:7. To God's honor Christ has accepted you!

15:9. I will praise thee, and sing praises to thy name!

15:10. Rejoice, ye nations!

15:11. Praise the Lord and glorify him!

12:15. *Rejoice* (with those who rejoice—including and especially the innocent little joys of life)!

12:12. Be joyful, rejoice (in the expectation of Jesus)!

Isn't chapter 8 pure joy? Thus there is—verse 1—no longer condemnation of those who are in Christ Jesus!!

O Emmy, don't we have pure cause for jubilation! Nothing but joy should be found in us. In Luke today, too, it said, REJOICE that your names are inscribed, that you are saved! Shall ever Satan or our sin or men take this joy away from us?

No, Emmy, John 16:22, "You will be joyful, and *no one* shall rob you of your joy." (NEB)

Ever joyful and happy is what I want you to be! There are so few Christians who are like that because most of the reborn do not understand the victorious looking to Christ, but keep looking inside themselves. That is the wretched life of Romans 7:7–24, a Christianity by law, from which Paul was long since freed. Compare verse 25, and chapters 6 and 8.

Now to the individual points: It is certainly very painful that you were bitter toward Frau Baehr, who after all has been an instrument of your conversion and a help in our engagement! But that is how we men all are. This *humbles* and *drives to Jesus*. He has forgiven you. However, in keeping with Matthew 5:23,24, I would in your place ask her for forgiveness for this and at the same time tell her that her trust is so

very important to you because you love her so much. That
therefore it was especially hurting to you that she did not
understand us, who wanted *only Jesus*. Thus the matter will
be thoroughly overcome, and of course in prayer. The other
you will find in the letter, which you yourself will please bring
to her as soon as ever possible so that she may read it in front
of you and discuss it with you. In Romans 15:2 it says that
we should strive to please our neighbors if *Jesus* is concerned
and if an offense is to be removed.

I shall answer Else today. It is very dear of you to be so
diligent with the poems! There is no hurry at all, however.
About Olga I was terrifically glad. Do you continue to have
those good impressions? Haslam and Finney are really books
full of amazing strength! Jesus, only Jesus, has done this. The
men (especially Haslam) were simple and weak.

Jesus will bless your letter to my sister Hannah very much.
I don't think she understands what Scripture calls "the world."
She thinks on the one hand of creation, the earth, every joy,
etc., and on the other hand of THE *evil* in the world, whereas
Scripture for the most part understands by it *un-reborn
mankind*. A more detailed explanation would lead too far
afield.

You are so right: "I feel myself so unworthy. Yet that is
just when Jesus can do something."

It is quite splendid that Mama is reading with Else. I am
terribly happy about that, and have honored Jesus very much.
We want to pray and believe! Jesus does miracles.

Emmy, *how* mercifully we are being led!

Pastor Meinhof's failure is very interesting, and not at all unexpected for me. He surely did not go about it biblically.

But imagine, Emmy, these days I am having serious doubts about my baptism theory, with strong inclination toward baptism of believers! The reason is not any single passage but the difficult question:

How can one imagine the strictly separated true Church (*Gemeinde*) of *believers* which Jesus and the apostles in actual fact wanted and carried out, if the practice of baptism is to be extended in my sense? Was not this extension, rather, already a defection from original Christianity? Since none of my explanations was a compelling proof *for* infant baptism, this shakes, almost takes by storm, my position, for I am in fact unclear and seeking! I almost feel convinced about baptism of believers. It came in prayer when I read, "Woe to them that seek to extinguish the light!" I said, "Lord, I never want to quench it, never to divert it! Show me what you want! I shall follow the light!" Then the sudden insight—so it seemed to me —came to me: You have quenched the light of understanding in the baptism question! Without *wanting* to.

Dear Emmy, all this is still unclear and perhaps wrong. Only one thing is certain: I must (in August) test the baptism question very thoroughly, and I am more determined than ever to obey, with no evasion.

But I wish to speak to NO ONE about it and have spoken to NO ONE. Such a matter must be *ripe* before it is spoken about. In questions of this kind, *that* sometimes takes a long time. Otherwise the development goes wrong. With the *Lord* we want to come to agreement; then we act, however it may be!

But now I must close, Emmy! The Lord protect you! I am very happy in the Lord and you, full of joy and peace!

Your faithful Ebbo

[From Eberhard to Emmy on a separate sheet of paper]

What advantage did the Jews have over the Gentiles?

I.

A great deal!

Above all, the Word of God is entrusted to them. It was accessible to all in the Temple and in the synagogue. And the Jews preserved it for the world forever, in accordance with God's will. Romans 3:1, 2.

But surely they did not have the true faith? No, but God's faithfulness is much greater than their unfaithfulness. They remained the people to whom the Word, the way to God, was entrusted. The blessing of circumcision was not taken from them. Before all nations, they had the *opportunity* to recognize God.

II.

None whatever!

The individual Jew was not saved through circumcision. He was under sin like the Gentile. Romans 3:9. Instead, he needed to experience the circumcision of the heart, to experience the rebirth out of the Spirit and the Word offered him. Only then did he have favor in God's sight and was one personally chosen by God. Romans 2:29.

In Col. 3:11, 12, baptism is called the circumcision of Christ.

Of what use was baptism by water?

I.

Very much!

To the baptized peoples (Churches) God's Word is entrusted. By them it is kept accessible to all for ever. All their members have opportunity to find God and Jesus if only they really seek. For everywhere the Word of God is offered them. Printed and spoken. Often debased, it is true, but Phil. 1:15–20. True, nominal Christians are in fact unbelievers. But Romans 3:3 remains so. Over and over again His Word comes close to them as distinct from the unbaptized peoples. The blessing of infant baptism is unmistakable! How much of our work would be *impossible* if we did not have the Christian religious instruction, however imperfect. Let us not scornfully reject this grace of God before the Gentiles, but let us give thanks!!

II.

None whatever!

The baptized individual remains under sin unless he is reborn out of the offered *Word* and the *Spirit*. He must be baptized with the Holy Spirit. Then the indication, the kind of baptism is carried out factually on his person. He believes and is baptized.

John baptizes (according to the Greek) toward repentance and forgiveness, thereby powerfully *pointing*, as pointer toward Christ. (→ †) Toward Christ. So too our baptism toward Christ (→) as pointer, toward (→), not INTO, death —as a pointer, as the mightiest imaginable challenge!

I shall break off here— I can't possibly go on writing. I am giving you this only for reflection.

My Ebbo,

I am happy about the way everything moves forward with us, the way Jesus more and more becomes Lord. My parents are getting used to it, in fact they are even showing interest. Mama says they love Else's "naive Bible explanations" very much, so that Papa too wants to have her give him a "Bible lesson" tomorrow evening or the next evening. Else doesn't think it matters if our parents are amused at first, as long as just one word stays with them. Heinz said yesterday that our conversion mania was a real stumbling block for him, that it left him no peace. The hymn "Almost Persuaded" was one he couldn't stand, but at the same time he always speaks about it. (Yesterday he said God had once created him when He was in a bad mood.) The minute I am particularly friendly to him, he says, "You don't want to convert me, do you?" It is plain to see that it doesn't leave him any peace anymore. Alwine [the maid] has also been converted. Even our char-woman, who at first always says, "No, all this praying the whole time!" has recently asked us to take her along to a meeting. I believe God is still going to do great things in Halle!

On Saturday evening I still went to Direktor Sievert's. We read together Joshua 1. Frau Sievert related this to baptism and said I should not yield either to the right or to the left (Joshua 1:7). This text has made up her mind to this. Fräulein von Nostiz got hold of Mimi on the street and said to her that God was speaking to her, and she should have herself baptized and not become stubborn. "Today if you hear his voice . . . ." (Heb. 3:7, NEB) I find it unbelievable. She surely means it well, but I am not a bit surprised that my parents are angry about it.

The Sallwürks even intend to withdraw directly from the established Church, to show their disagreement with it. The Sallwürks consider every clergyman a person who fights against God's Word.

Incidentally, the university lecturer Heim[14] visited us. He would like a contact with our family. He said he was a friend of Herr von Gerdtell's though in many things he thought differently. It seems he also spoke about you. Papa said, "Yes, now the baptizers have infiltrated this circle," to which Heim answered that this was not the main point. He stood up very much for the Fellowship.

Pray very much for me and everyone. For all of Halle we want to pray! I believe the much-discussed baptism is standing very much in the way.

Your faithful Emmy

Halle, June 18, 1907

My Ebbo,

Just now I received your long, detailed letter, which sends me very much into prayer. As I don't know how long I can write to you today, I would like to start right off with what is most important to me, that is, baptism. Just think, it has been similar with me! I have often thought, isn't baptism of believers also more biblical?

Yesterday I was at a Bible class at the Sallwürks, held by

---

[14] The Protestant theologian Karl Heim (1874–1958), later a friend of the Bruderhof.

Herr Westerhof. Herr von Sallwürk threw open the question, "What are sectarians? In Scripture there is a warning against them—Titus 3:10." Westerhof, who actually wanted to speak about Ephesians, said, "God is showing me now that we should take Romans 14." Then he said that sectarians are those who (like many here) do not stress the Cross of Jesus, for this is enough for us all, but they place other, secondary questions in the foreground, and make more laws, for example, baptism, Sabbath, and other things. We should stay away from such people lest the Cross be set at nought. *How does the Apostle act?* Paul is free from every law; with the Jews he is a Jew, with the Greeks he is a Greek. *Acts 16:3.* Not only from personal conviction! Even in Jerusalem, Acts 21:15–26. He does this only in wisdom, so as not to dampen the work.

Applying this to our question of baptism: This latter has been a setback for many souls 1) Henny Zabeler, 2) Fräulein Köhler, and some others (especially our parents and Heinz), who were very much moved. I think now: We are free from every law through Jesus! I believe we must do what He shows us, wherever He places us to work for Him, whether we are baptized or not. As above: Paul has Timothy circumcised (a sacrament instituted by God) only so that he can work for Jesus.

One other point that inclines me *toward* infant baptism is the promise: "Believe in the Lord Jesus Christ, and you and your household shall be saved." I believe that before I see it! Yet I don't want to say anything yet; God will show us! Pray for this; I am doing so too.

About me you need not be concerned; I make an effort to do everything to keep my health for Jesus and for you. I am already feeling better too. I believe too that I often brood too much and look too much at myself instead of at Jesus. I notice that it does not help me along. Your poem expresses it beautifully, and I am very happy about that. Only when I look to Him am I happy! Then I have joy and peace! What you write about this strengthens me very much.

I think what you write about Frau Baehr and to her is fine. I shall do that, and go to her either today or tomorrow, bring her the letter and speak with her. She does not understand our relationship at all.

I still wanted to write to you, by the way, about the Bible class yesterday, that it was richly blessed. Afterwards everyone recognized their faults, that they had looked away from Jesus too much and at lesser things, and had imagined themselves higher than others. This already follows from the fact that those who wanted to have themselves baptized were actually only interested in Else. No one was concerned about Olga and Mimi anymore.

May Jesus help me so that He grows greater in me. My trust in Him is firm as rock!

Your faithful Emmy

Halle, June 19, 1907

My Ebbo,

Olga's letter to you is really touching. I see the matter still somewhat differently, for, first, I am not clear yet whether I really acted correctly before God, although I wanted to; and second, I rejoice about it, for through this, Jesus draws me still closer to His heart; it humbles me very much, and I constantly ask myself, "Did you act as Jesus wants? If not, show it to me; I am ready to follow Thee and to put in order that in which I have failed." Thus I have to thank God for taking away my honor before children of God. For example, I recently received from a lady a paper or tract, "How is it with your conversion?" I also tested myself in this. The lady CERTAINLY meant very well. Still, perhaps she saw by my face that I was rather surprised. So she said, "You can also give it away." I find it very good if one often repeats one's conversion or surrender to God. You remember of course when we promised God together to sacrifice to Him all honor, even in the eyes of children of God, and already now the first time, I am defeated in such small things. I am ashamed for where I have sinned (and I certainly have sinned, especially when I was often somewhat touchy at first). I could give you several examples. Now I am concerned *only* that God understands me and forgives me where I have failed, knowingly or unknowingly. I am thankful that He humbles me! I do not want to lie, however; it is also *very* important to me that you also understand me. And you do, don't you, my Ebbo? I feel terrible about it that there is still so much sin in me. Else too is very loving to me. She finds it terrible that I am not understood in many things, and she wants to do as much as she can. She is really so sweet. She has now gone to Frau Doktor Schulze about it. She reproaches me for not justifying myself more; I cannot do that, however, until I know that I have acted rightly. O Ebbo, pray that God discloses everything to me! And if not, then He will cover it up or else show that I tried to do His will.

Always your faithful Emmy

Breslau, June 20, 1907

They follow the Lamb wherever He goes! Rev. 14:4.
My Emmy,

Yes, that is how it must be, and so it is, too! I am so *very*
happy about your letters, for many reasons, above all because
I see how you are becoming ever happier because ever more
free through Him, for Him! I too am indescribably happy,
full of love and strength in Jesus, as in the strongest time of
my life. I can say and shall say it over and over that you, my
bride, have drawn me mightily upwards. From the beginning,
you are a deep blessing, and have brought me much nearer to
Jesus!

Before I ever knew you, I often feared that we could be
drawn downwards some day—as so many are. "Then never!"
I often said to the Lord at that time.

But Hallelujah, now I need no longer be afraid! You are
the human being through whom I have the mightiest and
deepest blessing! Thank Jesus for this and ask Him to make
you *more and more* a blessing! We want, you and I both, to
be always ready to help each other, to bring each other forward, to strengthen and call each other to watchfulness—
whatever is needed at the time!

You are so right: *total love to Jesus makes us indifferent to
praise and rebuke!* You know, I often find praise harder than
blame and misunderstanding because I see more temptation
in it. I also rejoice with thanks about misunderstanding and
slights from children of God, however dear they are, because
I know that this humbling is good for me. If Jesus is every-

thing to us, that is so easy! I hope Olga will also see that; she wrote so extremely lovingly.

But we must hold fast to this—disrespectful misunderstanding of true people of Jesus stems from evil just as much as the disgusting honoring of men. *Of both,* children of God must be *thoroughly* cleansed. And there you, my heart, have a task! I believe you yield too much to the weaknesses of your sisters! I am acquainted with this disrespectful misunderstanding from my days with the Salvation Army, when in the end I was regarded everywhere with pity, by some because I had not kept my word and had not gone through with it and by others because I had chosen unspiritual, unhealthy erroneous ways. All this just after I had stood—WITHOUT ANY divine justification—on the heights of conspicuous admiration; for me a very good contrast. Here two things became important to me. One is the lowly humbling in the joy of Jesus (see page 1 of this letter—the text), but also the second, the task with children of God. Emmy, JESUS IS IN YOU! You must glorify HIM! He is dishonored, however, if you silently allow others to doubt in your devotion to Him. Those children of God who have been diverted from the banner "Jesus only!" are the very ones to whom you must ever again joyfully witness that Jesus is everything to you, how you serve Him alone, and what He gives you. We don't want to stir up the points of argument; yet the more points of argument there are, the more unfeigned and the more undimmed shall be our glorifying of Him!! Thus I think you should be less tempted, more innocent, more untroubled in confessing to Jesus and only Jesus, and stressing the fellowship in Him! In this way He will be glorified and the offenses will vanish. (As already now at home!) Jesus is grieved when you children of God do not have full, free trust in one another. Therefore pray and act so that this will be overcome! You understand what I mean by emphasizing the other side? I believe you have a great task *from the Lord,* in a very unsensational way. Fulfill it before you have to leave. I am praying for that and know you will succeed.

I rejoice very much that you have made such a good beginning with our dear Frau Baehr. Her letter is really nice! Please send it back to me, and tell her I was *very* happy with it!

Unfortunately I must close. I always want to pour out my whole heart to you right away!

Your Ebbo

Pure Service

O Lord, hear this one request of mine—
Spoken from the depths of my heart.
Let every step of faith I venture
Be taken to honor Thee alone!

I know Thou workest mighty deeds
Through me, as through each one who believes;
Broad fields stand ready for the harvest—
The Foe is robbed of his victory.

But Lord, give Thy pure and holy blessing!
Let self be completely given over to death,
May every brother lay down
His honor before Thee, and Thee alone!

Yes, Lord, this one thing Thou must grant:
Not even a shadow of fame for me.
For Thee, Thee only, my poor life,
Thy possession to Thy glory!

Destroy, O Lord, our human sin
That robs Thee of Thy holy glory!
Let no one make so bold anymore
To honor a fellowman who simply believes!

O prove to us in holy clearness
How wretched we are in Thy sight;
How far from Thy truth he is
Who finds ground and cause for praise in man!

Make all human glory nothing
Through Thy holy majesty.
May Thy Spirit show Thee so mighty
That all praise of men shall be dispelled!

E. A. June 21, 1907

Halle, June 21, 1907

*The eyes of the Lord pass through the whole earth to prove
His might in those who with undivided heart are directed
to Him!*

My Ebbo,

Your letter today made me very happy. It is really wonderful that we are so completely one in our Savior and are
becoming so more and more, the more fully we love Him.

Our whole life a praising of His glory! Yet I notice that I still lack a *great* deal. Only as long as I look entirely away from myself to Him is it possible!

I am so happy that God always bestows such unspeakable blessing on me through you and that you always draw me higher, to Him. You are after all much further along than I, and it is good if you tell me everything! For we really want to see our life in such a way that we constantly help each other forward to become more like Him!

When you write to me that you think it disgraces Jesus if one does nothing to prevent other children of God from doubting my dedication to Him, you are surely right. I had not looked at it from that angle. I only did not want to seek my own credit since I so easily tend to justify myself. I believe that if I always look toward Him, I will succeed in glorifying Him, also without seeking honor for myself in any way.

This morning we received in the mail from Pastor Meinhof "Justification of Infant Baptism," written by himself. At 6 o'clock today there will be another lecture by him in the parish house. Everybody is going. Even complete outsiders and unconverted people are concerning themselves with the question, "Is infant baptism valid, or shall we have ourselves baptized?" We have already experienced two cases in the best circles of Halle. It is getting to be "the style" now, it seems. I shall go at 6 o'clock today too.

I thought it would be better to present the personal Savior to the children without using the word "conversion" and to tell them a lot about Jesus and His love, *not* as is usual in children's services, "You shall not lie, not steal, not eat sweets on the sly." I think one should *rather*, or *altogether only*, stress the positive side instead of the negative, for every human being would rather receive or possess something than give up something for Jesus' sake. How can they ever give anything up for His sake when they don't have Him at all?

I am already looking forward very much to your next letter, and I hope very much that you will tell a lot about yourself. That is the main thing for me. I always pray that God may bless you for all men with whom He brings you together, and then for all your studies, and for your and my understanding in the baptism question. I actually believe I must have myself baptized; still it is not clear to me whether this is human influence or divine recognition, and therefore I am still waiting and praying a great deal for this. I believe our Savior does not send these questions requiring decision for nothing. One has to take an attitude to it.

Just now there is a really dreadful storm, lightning and thunder, hail, and hurricane such as I have never seen. In front of our house alone five big trees have been torn up, and at the fairgrounds, merry-go-rounds were knocked over. God speaks so plainly, but natural man perceives nothing of God's Spirit.

But I must close. You too, pray very much for me, for my work for the Savior; and I need still much more Holy Spirit to guide me into all truth, to give me much more clarity about myself and my sins and weaknesses. It makes Jesus appear much greater when we ourselves are so powerless. I would like to say with Paul, "If boasting there must be, I will boast of the things that show up my weakness." (2 Cor. 11:30, NEB) His power is mighty in the weak.

Now greet everyone very much. Olga received a card from Hannah today. What is Betty doing?

Your ever faithful Emmy

Halle, June 22

My Ebbo,

Today I only want to write quite briefly. I look forward to Monday and your letter.

Here in Halle there is great excitement about yesterday's hurricane. Many thought the end of the world had come. At the fairgrounds, where before there was such life and activity, everything was laid waste and destroyed within half an hour! Clothing material, huts, toys, wooden framework flew over roofs. Trees were uprooted and injured or killed people. This picture of misery, of devastation—everybody stood stupefied with sad faces in front of piles of rubbish from which hardly anything could be saved. Else and I, without any respect of persons, went through the fair with tracts we had recently received from Stenzel: 1) What is human life? 2) Chance, or God's will? 3) (And so on, all of it very pertinent). We gave out 70 tracts. Everyone received them with great gratitude. One could hear cries like "We were almost gone," or "Yes, what is life?" It was really heartbreaking. God showed His omnipotence! There was nothing man could do.

Yesterday I was at the baptism discussion. It was a hot debate! Pastor Meinhof against six speakers, including two Baptists. Professor Riehm here spoke *for* baptism of believers.

Just about all of Halle was there! A few declared, *"On the basis of Scripture I must have myself baptized."* Frau Baehr, the Sallwürks, and Fräulein von Nostiz were there too. The struggle lasted nearly two and a half hours.

Tomorrow afternoon I am invited to L. Franke's. Today Papa received a *very* nice letter from Pastor Fabianke. I can come, if not now, then later. Hannah also wrote me again *very* nicely. It is not clear to her how that is, to live *only* for Jesus. She wonders whether one would do nothing but pray, read the Bible or religious things, and speak about Him. Then one could go into a monastery, I should think. To live in the world is just what a Christian should do, only doing everything *for Him* and *with Him.* That is what I think.

Your faithful Emmy

Breslau, June 23, 1907

My Emmy,

Everything in Jesus and through Jesus.

Today I could again write you many, many pages, but because Clara is here, I must limit myself somewhat.

All that you write about baptism is very important to me. I believe Pastor Meinhof is doing the baptism movement more good than a lot of propaganda. To me it seems almost completely sure that baptism of believers is early-Christian and biblical. But Emmy, the question is very complicated, and we must test it slowly and objectively *in quiet trust.* Mainly, let us say *nothing* until we have an incontestably firm clarity. I also consider it possible that God is intentionally leaving quite unclear the question as to *when* and *how* baptism should be done, so as not to detract from the faith in Jesus alone. It is remarkable how Bible *and* history are conspicuously silent on this point! Now, I am going to search honestly and thoroughly, recognize what is willed by God, and act accordingly. In either case, whether this way or that, we shall not let our center be displaced by one millimeter: *We need Jesus alone, and nothing else!*

Hannah's question moves me all the more since she wrote similarly to Clara. Let us praise and give thanks—she wishes to be *whole*! Your viewpoint is quite right. Only take great care that the Enemy does not use it to weaken something. I fear this in the case with Clara. I think you must show Hannah that to use *everything, everything, utterly* FOR *Jesus alone*, is MUCH *more* than to limit one's sphere of activity like a nun! It demands tremendous energy from God to assimilate into oneself modern science and literature, society and decadent culture, and to work it through inwardly in such a way that nothing comes out but *Jesus*—that is, for *souls*! This Hannah must realize; she is in the world *to win souls* for Jesus, to bring to Him as many hearts as possible, *whole and undivided. Everything* that goes contrary to this goal, or even does not serve it, must be resolutely rejected.

God bless you for Hannah!! I pray very much. You, especially *Else* and *you*, but Mimi as well, have a great task from the Lord to help her. Make faithful use of it, and write to her very often!

What you say about the positive side and dedication is very right. *Jesus*, the complete Christ of the Bible, is what people must get to know. Only when they know Him can they become free. However, we do not want the Cross of discipleship to be covered over with flowery vines, either. The Cross is the most important part of the picture of Jesus. He gives all and demands all. Dying and living, totality of self-denial, and triumph of new life—*this is He*, and these are His people. Him we want to proclaim and exemplify, the Crucified and Risen One.

That children can be converted is a certainty to me. The expression makes no difference. I would apply every means to help them to understand that Jesus wants them complete, He, who alone loves them completely.

Imagine—2 Corinthians 12:9, with Galatians 6:14, is in a certain way my best-loved text! I praise God for using us both in *this* way! About Alwine's conversion I am very happy. Greet her, please. Let us hope the cleaning woman will also soon come to "all this praying the whole time." That is splendid that you were able to give out tracts! It was so "given" in the situation! I think God has spoken powerfully. Oh, if they would only allow their empty frivolity to be destroyed by Him, and be saved! Sometimes such events have been an omen or an affirmation of an awakening. May God grant it over Halle!

Doktor Heim's visit interested me very much. He is a dear person and wants to follow Jesus. For me he is too soft as a man, and as a Christian too indulgent. I should like to know what he has said about me.

Because of shortage of time, I can only write you about Romans 9–11 that the point at issue here is God's freewilling choice in the use of instruments. Jacob He used, Esau He did not. Pharaoh's hardening was a tool of God's. Israel, the people of the Covenant, is God's tool out of God's free choice in the history of His salvation, and so on. It is connected, but it is *not* the same as the saving and rejection of souls! Romans 9–11 is historical, the historical plan of salvation.

This week I was able to speak for Jesus twice. First in the German S.C.M. on Wednesday, about "Will and Deed." We went through the whole New Testament on the basis of this question. *Jesus* was among us, and the leader said at the end that it had been a long time since we had a class like that. May God give them all the will to act, through Jesus!!

A nice bank messenger who is converted, formerly a cobbler, asked me for a talk. This friend has confidence in me since 1903, when as a complete stranger I walked into his cobbler shop with the *War Cry*[15] and challenged his master and him to give themselves completely to Jesus.

This week I was at my dear Major Catherine Bissmeyer's who commissioned me to hold the consecration meeting in the Salvation Army next Sunday. At table I mentioned the Major as my friend, and then Mama told about a professor's son who is a "ne'er-do-well"—I know him. He came home with the Salvation Army insignia and stated that he was now going to save souls. His father, horrified, thereupon sent him to the country, as a gardener, I believe, where he was supposed to prove himself as a new man. With Mama I can discuss everything; however, she does not become converted, but just says, "The good boy!" Papa is somewhat more difficult again. A clear witness from me recently made him very angry; but he asked me not to tell you about it since he was ashamed of quarreling with his son.

Your Ebbo

[15] Magazine of the Salvation Army.

Halle, June 23, 1907
9 p.m. o'clock

My Ebbo,

I also believe that the main development of my dedication to God has of course taken place *after* my engagement. Quite decidedly I have received the *very greatest* blessing from you, and through you it first became clear to me, and has become ever clearer, what it means "to live for Jesus and to be there for Him." We both want to ask God *very* much that He will go on giving me more and more blessing through you and that you will show me everything that I must put aside in order to be completely filled with Him.

Before our engagement I did not know yet what I was really doing in giving myself over to Jesus. Because I recognized Jesus' love and truth—that is why I did it. But it would be lying if I said I had felt great sins. It often made me uneasy that only after my conversion, not even until weeks afterwards, was I worried about sins. If I read, for example, that others felt so unhappy about the burden of their sin and found peace in breaking down under the Cross, this made me confused about my conversion. I now believe, however, that God takes each person differently. This became clear to me through various of your books, and through your letters too. I want to write this to you again so that you may know quite exactly how I am thinking.

Your always faithful Emmy

Halle, June 25, 1907

My Ebbo,

Your letter yesterday made me immensely happy. I shall first answer it, and then write the other things to you.

About baptism I still do not have a really definite concept. Just one thing I do know: I personally have not had *anything* from my baptism as an infant. I don't feel the slightest blessing coming from it. I came to God through my conversion, not through baptism.

Next Friday at 3:30 o'clock the great baptism is to take place. There are quite a number who are going to be baptized: 1) the Sallwürks, 2) Frau Vogler, 3) the Sieverts, 4) Herr Zornow, 5) a deaconess, 6) Dönitz, I believe; and several from out of town besides. Else is steadily praying that she too will be allowed. Shall I do it too? Is it right, do you think? Often I think yes, but then again no, for I have recently heard of some people who have been baptized four or five times. In such a question, however, it is *wrong* to discuss it with flesh and blood; instead one must *recognize* and *act*. If God shows me clearly that I should do it, I shall definitely dare to do so. If I have myself baptized, I shall be thrown out of the house. Still, this shall not be what determines me.

Hannah moves me also very much; she wants to be *whole.* You are right in writing that my point of view may be used by the Devil. May that never be! Yet, Ebbo, I would be lying if I said, for example, "I shall now go for a walk for Jesus." This is what I think: I go walking with Jesus, and am completely at His disposal. I might go to the Peissnitz Island, for example, but I pay attention to whether He intends something else for me, perhaps in meeting other people. So I let myself be led by Him, and this is how it is with everything. Yet if I say I do everything directly *for* Jesus, then I can't do anything but pray and save souls. Although I always want this and stand ready for it, still I also do other things, for example of course

I sleep, and I converse with unconverted people as well, like my parents, without always speaking about Jesus. Indirectly I do it for Jesus, but still not directly. That would be self-delusion, therefore self-deception, a tremendous lie! In the morning I always pray: Lord, the day belongs to Thee; lead me together with those through whom Thou canst bless me or others; I am at Thy disposal. Another example: When we were in Breslau together and went walking or boating, we were with Jesus, but still *not for* Jesus. We rejoiced in Him. How do you see that? Or am I not standing right? Please write that to me!

Your Emmy

Breslau, June 26, 1907

Psalm 150!

My Emmy,

My heart is full of rejoicing, praise, and thanks. There is continuously such a joy in me about our mighty Lord and about my bride.

A great deal in your letters has moved me most deeply, and requires a detailed answer. Today I can only answer everything fragmentarily, even if it is to be made understandable only by my Sunday letter.

The deep split through the baptism question happens frequently, a proof for many children of God that the present-day conflicts originate with the Enemy. *Please* try through Frau Baehr to heal this wound in the children of God in Halle! John 17.

In regard to baptism, stand firm in the peace of Jesus!! Do

not press the Lord. His silence is an answer, that is, "No" for now. I believe the baptism atmosphere in Halle is having too strong an effect on you for you to be able to decide calmly and objectively. Wait, then, in faith and in dedication!

I consider indirect action for Jesus *just as* important as the direct, if the latter is also clearly present. If you do not sleep and do not go for walks, etc., you sin against your body and make yourself unusable for Jesus' service. Thus you do it *for Him*. If you were to speak to your parents ONLY about Jesus, conversion, the Bible, and so on, you would have no access to their hearts whatsoever after a few days. Your response to their interests, joys, and sorrows is therefore the most necessary and most important service you can do them. You do it *for Jesus!* From both these and similar examples it follows that our boat rides and walks were also entirely *for Jesus*.

But I am happy about how the Lord leads. I am much happier, more joyful, and more trusting in Jesus' leading. I am full of peace to know that the Lord is blessing you there and me here, and *His leading is the best*.

Now may Jesus bless you with streams of joy and strength! Praying with great joyfulness for you,

Your Eberhard

Halle, June 27, 1907

My Ebbo,

I shall let the opportunity for baptism pass tomorrow unless God tells me directly, "Go there." I hope the conflicts among the children of God will now end.

I am very happy that your studies are going along so well

and that you do everything *only for Jesus*. I must first think it over whether this is so with me too. That you now work only until 10:15 I find *very* good. I am very happy about that.

Else has just come home with the news that several more have been added to those who are to be baptized tomorrow. For Else, too, everything is in readiness. So far, however, there is as yet no possibility that she will be allowed to. She is praying unceasingly. I am also praying that she may be allowed, for I consider it right. Emma at Frau Baehr's is also having herself baptized. I keep wondering whether I should do it?

It would be very nice if some time you would write to Papa. He always is *very* glad for it. Don't write anything about the baptism, however, before everything is clear to you, indisputably clear.

Your faithful Emmy

Halle, June 28, 1907

My Ebbo,

I believe you will be very angry if I tell you something. Yesterday, after the Alliance meeting, which was held by the baptizing preacher and was much blessed, there was a big discussion about today's baptism. (Until now twelve persons have announced themselves for baptism.) Afterwards I was walking a little way with Frau Baehr alone. We also came to the topic of baptism. I told her I was not quite clear yet, but I had a strong inclination toward baptism of believers, and about you I also said that you were thinking over your concept of baptism but that nothing was clear to you yet. Of course Frau Baehr will not speak about this. Thereupon Frau Baehr almost exulted and said it was God's answer to prayer, that she had prayed for us, especially for you, for illumination on this point. And she worked on me to have myself baptized today after all. She asked what was still standing in my way and said that one must *obey*. 1) Are you angry with me for saying that about you? It was not right, since of course you did not want it; it was thoughtlessness. Please answer this, quite briefly. It troubles me *very* much. 2) Today I have no idea what the will of God in this matter is. Earlier Else asked to be allowed to be baptized, and I said I was also thinking of it. Of course there was again an uneasy atmosphere. The rest I will write to you tomorrow.

I am really sad that I said that about you.

Your faithful Emmy

Halle, *June 29*

My Ebbo,

You know, Albert Still writes very nicely. He too, however, is doing rather a lot of recruiting for baptism. It seems to be that way everywhere here. Herr von Gerdtell's card is extremely nice. Yesterday at the coffee party this movement was naturally discussed too (they were all worldly ladies). I was amazed about how little people understood of it. They of course attacked Herr von Gerdtell and said he had begun "the baptism thing" in Halle. I was very much upset inwardly, but I looked only toward Jesus and then said quite quietly, "I also belong to this movement, and I am very glad about what Jesus has done in Halle to me and others." Something like that.

Your faithful Emmy

Halle, June 29, 1907

My Ebbo,

Today I didn't go to the Bible class or for a walk either after all, as Mama didn't want me to go at all. Toward evening Else and I went to Brother Stenzel's, where we had a little Bible class. He told us a lot about yesterday's baptism, which they say did not take place until about 9 o'clock, at Cämern, in a secluded little wood. It was really wonderful—toward evening there was all at once a big rainbow in the sky. Gen. 9:12–17.

I believe the children of God blame in particular Frau Doktor Schulze and us for not being present. Frau Doktor Schulze is against it and has already been misunderstood a great deal on account of it.

You know, my Ebbo, I don't know whether it is quite right. It seemed to me as if some of the baptizers were rather over-excited. I noticed it the evening before last. For example, Frau Direktor Sievert said she was so happy, it was like Christmas, and she felt like climbing up a pole for joy. And Else kept standing before Frau Baehr, asking her: Do pray that I may be allowed; you can pray that my legs may be cut off and my eyes lost if this helps me to come to baptism. Then I said, how-ever, that I considered it a sin to say anything like that for the sake of baptism. God can do it a different way too if He wants. I was apparently not understood, though. O Ebbo, if we perhaps are baptized, let us ask especially for a holy quiet-ness, a holy peace beforehand. I find that horrible! One can of course understand this joy in being able now to carry out the will of God as they have recognized it. Do you think this joy is the Holy Spirit? And I have only a little and perhaps do not understand it? This has also caused me to think.

One other thing that I often wonder about. Will perhaps only the baptized be bodily removed to Heaven? Do only they belong to the Bride-Church? Have you ever thought about that? Rev. 14:1b. They had a sign on their forehead. Is it baptism? I look forward very much to your next letter. Today I think constantly of March 29. How happy we are! Psalm 34:17. Eph. 1:14b.

I must close, however, for we shall eat soon.

Everyone greets you very much. Please greet your dear parents and Betty very warmly. Tomorrow I shall write to Clara.

In faithful love in Jesus,

Your bride

Breslau, June 29, 1907

My Emmy,

I hasten to reassure you. I am *not at all* very angry, my child, *not the tiniest bit* at all.

I believe it comes from your great love for me that you easily begin speaking about me and what concerns me.

This does not prevent me, however, my Emmy, from finding it wrong that you are not able to control yourself more. It is very disagreeable to me to have very immature, incomplete reflections of mine become known, for I wish to represent *only* what I am *thoroughly* convinced of. Please tell this also to Frau Baehr, to whom I am *very* thankful for her intercession. You know that baptism is quite unclear to me, that it might take years until I have formed a conviction in regard to it, and that this may turn out to the right *and* to the left—either-or.

I did not find it right, either, that you told Elisabeth Franke about our engagement without agreeing on it with me beforehand. Let us please keep strictly to that! In this way all rash steps will be avoided.

In this case, now that it has happened, I am more or less in agreement since I understand your need and I see a certain justification, although so far I admit I am not convinced of the *necessity*. Well, my Emmy, *but don't be sad!*

Your faithful Ebbo

Jesus wants to have you *joyful*, and so does your Ebbo. You do, don't you, always bring little things like this to the Lord in thanks for His forgiveness and purification.

In your place I would say nothing about your inclination toward baptism, for you are of course quite unclear. Consequently there can be no question of obedience either. On the contrary, without an indisputably firm, deeply founded conviction it would be *sin, a grave sin!* Rom. 14:23!

Please do not withdraw from Fräulein L.F.! On the contrary, show her as much love as possible!

Breslau, June 29–30, 1907

My Emmy,

The Lord will give me strength—I am praying for it. And all the more so if we get as old as a Salvation Army sister wished me today, that is 100 years, so that I might be able to work for a really long time.

Just now I returned home from the powerfully blessed meeting. The dear Major gave me the entire leadership. The numerous gathered Salvation Army members greeted me with loud Hallelujahs and beaming faces. After we had several times prayed on our knees and I had told something about Halle, of course about you all too without mentioning names, I spoke about Romans 6:11, 13 in the strength of the Spirit, whom I had received in prayer from the Lord. The meeting was mightily moved—practically only converted people were there. Many confessed to unfaithfulness, some broke down sobbing violently; altogether the spirit of prayer had laid hold of their hearts. Emmy, it was glorious how Jesus again has heard and used His most worthless servant. I have seldom experienced anything like it. I myself was moved to the depths, *but continued to conduct the meeting in quiet confidence.* Many had become very excited, in Salvation-Army fashion, *so I admonished to peace and quietness before God.* The chief thing, however, was that God's Spirit showed up sin, clearly and sharply, in the most varied and hidden forms, and that almost all the dear souls took hold of full saving in Jesus. Jesus preserve the blessing! And He will do it. At the end, the meeting praised and honored our great Lord.

My Bible and your letters are to me the most precious things in my room.

Baptism seems to concern you mightily. Of course it is not the sign in Revelation 14:1b. All who overcome through the Word, that is, all who are reborn, who love the Word in faith and obedience according to their understanding, receive the name of God on their foreheads. Rev. *3:7–12.* No *particular* condition for the bodily removal is given, except this one: *that of being in Christ.* 1 Thess. 4:16, 17.

To me the agitation about baptism does not seem right—therefore not of the Holy Spirit. Else's excited declarations are unnecessary, senseless, and wrong—therefore not of the Holy Spirit. The Lord can do what He wants, and He likes best to do it when all our own fire is put to work for it.

My position has become clearer, and this happened yesterday. Stimulated by the text from you which I have put up over my desk, I drafted the enclosed poem, at the same time thinking of our possible baptism and equally as much of the persecutions of the end-time. Afterwards I rode to a quiet wood to reflect about it and to pray. I want to stress three points:

I. 1) Under all circumstances I shall do the clearly recognized will of God.

2) I shall do nothing except what I am convinced of after examining it from all sides.

3) I shall not step forward with anything that I cannot clearly verify as biblical, and can therefore justify precisely to all.

II. From my impressions at this moment, three things follow for the near future:

1) I shall search through the New Testament and history for the baptism question, quite objectively.

2) Should my present impression be confirmed that baptism of believers could be more biblical, that is, *alone biblical,* I shall have myself baptized as soon as I have it *quite firm scholastically* (according to the Bible and history).

3) At the same time I shall then publish three little books on *Gemeinde*, conversion, and baptism in early Christian times.

III. The practical outcome is this:

1) I can *not* be baptized *now* without sinning.

2) My private studies after my two exams will be devoted to the questions of *Gemeinde* and baptism.

3) I shall *probably* be baptized after about three years; about this, however, I *can* and *will* say NOTHING definite before concluding my studies. Silence, therefore!

More about my plan of work. If all goes well then, I hope in March 1909 to be a candidate in theology with the degree of Doctor of Philosophy (and also officially your bridegroom). Then I shall immediately get to work to publish within a year three booklets that belong together inwardly and are to be followed by others, perhaps according to the following plan:

ORIGINAL CHRISTIANITY

Booklets toward understanding the apostolic times.

I. The wholeness (purity) of the original Christian Church communities.

II. Conversion in original Christianity.

III. Early Christian baptism.

———

IV. The apostolic witness.

V. The gifts of original Christianity.

VI. Early Christian organization.

Therefore, in case I should accept baptism of believers as alone right on the basis of my research, I will make my step effective *by this alone*. I must be the one who proves that it is the calm, clearly reasoned conviction of the will of Jesus and the apostles that has brought me to baptism. Otherwise people will be quick to say, "*Ach*, first the Salvation Army! Now baptism! Always going to extremes! That comes from his temperament."

No, whatever I do, I want to do it *with full force*. And to me it is quite clear that this way (clear motivation for every action) is the will of the Lord. Should I gain my former conviction through my studies, well and good, I shall then verify infant baptism, etc. IN EITHER CASE *I shall act quite calmly, objectively, without judging others, without pushing Jesus from the center.*

My great wish is of course that you not be baptized before me, but with me, *if the Lord leads it so*. All this, my Emmy, is of course only for you and shall be said TO NO ONE for now.

Do write to me what you think of "For Jesus." It is a very natural directing *of all things* toward the one goal. I have thanked God terrifically for the way my love has become a blessing to you. You know it is the same way with me.

Then I still wanted to write to you that I always love you *very specially* when you tell me something that bothers you or in which I should help you, as recently with telling things to others. My Emmy, we want to continue always telling each other everything, even if it is hard for us. That is the only kind of relationship I consider ideal and right, that you tell me and I tell you everything.

Next week I shall above all prepare my sermon, which I am to hold on July 13 on Matthew 21:28–32. I shall make two parts:

1) Christendom, not rest but work!

2) The Kingdom of God consists not in words but in strength. Not words, but action!

In the past week I have had to struggle a good deal inwardly:

I have sometimes had serious worries (see poem!) when thinking of *both* of our *beloved* parents, in the event that we should have ourselves baptized. I see this as extremely serious and feel very much afraid, out of love to them.

O Emmy, pray that I may ever hold very firm to faith. *He does not lead us on wrong ways!* For we are careful and biblical in obeying Jesus alone. *And His way is blessing for all.* I have been very much warned to caution by an experience, *like many others,* in which a certain one claims he has divine certainty that he should become a Catholic priest. Very interesting and instructive! I can unfortunately only send you the accompanying lines of the Assessor Jeremias [a State official] from Dresden.

We do not want to obey inner voices and feelings, and such things, but to *stand on the Word, the Scripture,* as it reveals itself to us in thorough, obedient searching. See for example John 15:10b.

I have been concerned about the dear students who took it mighty ill of me that I attend the meetings so little.

Wanting always to show you my whole weak heart and trusting you,

Ebbo

Breslau, July 2, 1907

Galatians 5:22

But the *fruit* of the *Spirit*
   is: *love, joy, peace, patience,*
     kindness, friendliness, faith,
     gentleness, chastity.

Here is something out of my old wallet. I just found this from 1899 (or 1900) in a little notebook of mine. Wonderful for us, isn't it?

My dear Emmy,

It is surely the Lord's will if I express to you today directly from my lecture my great deep joy about your letter. I went back home in the hour between lectures today especially to pray and to read your letter.

How clearly you express that I should always tell you everything. And what a noble concept of love you express. JUST as *I* think. You know, I *must* say it, I look up to you *with reverence.* Because of this it is always so *very* hard for me to tell you anything that I don't think is right. But you can rely on this forever: *I will under all circumstances tell you everything about yourself and everything about myself.* I only would wish that you would find more in *me* that I need to change. It is *certainly* much more necessary in my case than in yours.

In my Sunday letter too, I only meant the *form,* the expression, in which I want to become ever less harsh, ever more loving. I thank you that you did not find the form too harsh either!

You know, I must above all rebuke and warn myself very much. Pray *very* much with me, my heart.

I believe that with Sister Marie you have little guilt or

none whatever. Surmises we can hardly prevent. *Lying we shall not do at any price,* in words or otherwise. *If this should be necessary for a concealment, we shall then make the engagement known* IMMEDIATELY. However, we *need* not try to deceive anyone, "I am not engaged"; instead, we only want to leave people in complete UNCERTAINTY as much as possible. For me here it is not so difficult as for you. For your brother Heinz I shall pray very much.

Baptism with water *is* neither baptism of the Spirit nor dying and resurrection. This causes disappointments or illusions.

You are right: *I do not need to write* YOU *that I have nothing to hide.* I am *so happy* about that. To be angry and let fly at you is something, I believe *surely,* I will NEVER be able to do. To *forgive* you sounds to me like arrogance on my part. Of course I do it *most completely,* and you to me also.

Now be very *very joyful* and write that to me! HE HAS JOY IN FULLNESS. *He* also gives you and me strength *to live completely for Him,* however far I and you too are still removed from the ideal. Looking forward to August,

Your bridegroom

P.S. I look forward tremendously to your poems!!

A printed copy of the poem *"Dank und Gelübde"* ("Thanks and a Vow") was enclosed in the above letter. In the margin Eberhard wrote:

July 1, 1907. Doesn't Kühn do quite lot of changing?[16]

Your happy Ebbo

[16] This is the way Bernhard Kühn altered the last four verses of Eberhard's poem, "O Jesus Savior," when he published it in the *Evangelical Alliance News.* For the original version see pp. 38–39.

Thanks and a Vow

O Thou great Master, be praised
For Thy Spirit's holy strength,
Which has shown me the way to the Cross,
Where God makes a new creation.

Whoever looks at the Cross, *must* conquer,
For there everything is overcome.
There we cannot be defeated;
The power of sin is forced to yield.

Thou hast given Thy blood for me
I too shall die with Thee!
O Hallelujah! I may live
For Thee with every breath I take!

So shall this be true then forever:
I myself no longer live, no—
Thou, holy One, would dwell within me,
I remain Thine in the radiance of the Cross.

E.A.

Halle, July 3, 1907

My Ebbo,

Today I received your dear letter. I am writing to you that
I am now again completely happy in my Lord and in you.
That you will tell me *everything*, no matter what it is, always
makes me very happy. Only thus can we help each other to
become like Jesus! In regard to Sister Marie I am surely also
at fault. Ebbo, it becomes ever clearer to me that everything,

whether in myself or other people—everything that is not Jesus is sin and nothing. In myself I notice it most plainly. We want always to pray very much for us both. He has made us so endlessly happy that we cannot do other than to thank!

Your faithful Emmy

Breslau, July 4, 1907

My Emmy,

Your letter is again an overflowing source of joy for me. You are right, we cannot do otherwise than *thank*! To Jesus be praise!! In Him loving you EVER MORE,

Your Ebbo

Breslau, July 5, 1907

In thy presence is fullness of joy! Psalm 16:11

My bride,

You cannot guess the worth of your pages today to me! Yes, *in His presence is fullness of joy!* If we quite ruthlessly uncover and do away with all evil, then *His peace is like a stream of water!*

He knows, too, that you are such a great blessing to me that I cannot give enough thanks for that. *He* is my God, and therefore for me He is above you in every respect. But you are the greatest thing He has given me. Oh, my prayer is that in everything you can have nothing but joy in me! I am quite incapable of this, but *He can help!*

I too want to do Jesus' will completely in regard to our letters. When I began speaking about that today, my parents again had nothing against it, the way it so often goes. I believe, however, it will be better if *later* we *send* them off less often; Jesus will give me strength to be always happy just the same. Therefore I shall go back to our *old agreement*. You keep to this always, but also the way Jesus shows it, if for me or for you it is just then an important strengthening. Under all circumstances we shall hold *firmly to this, that we tell each other everything that is of any importance at all*. I am sure Jesus wants it. Perhaps later we will write something every day, put it together, and then send it off twice a week? We will save that way too. However, we don't want to make any law for ourselves, but rather to be free for the leading of the Spirit. My feeling is that we can just leave it that way until we can talk it over in August and then see further.

I shall be quite overjoyed when we talk everything over!
Again quite happy in Jesus and you!

Your Eberhard

Halle, July 6, 1907

My Ebbo,

It is *our happiness,* after all, that we want to bear everything together, and quite especially what is hard. For this we want always to thank Jesus!

At home it is not easy now either. At every occasion Else and I get to hear things like, "It is absolute hypocrisy to say that you want to do everything for Jesus." Olga too makes it hard for us often. Still we are happy in Him for whose sake we are allowed to suffer! These days I am dead tired from it all; pray that I may receive more strength to carry and that I am able to sleep at night. I always pray for you, and just now again that Jesus may give you *much* strength for your work and in general. Ebbo, I long to be able to talk everything over with you.

Your faithful Emmy

Breslau, July 6, 1907 (Sunday)
In thy presence is fullness of joy!

My Emmy,

I just want above all to write you that I am now again unceasingly happy in my Jesus! Last night and this morning I had deep hours of blessing in which He was very close to me and I talked over your last letters completely with Him. The last one in particular was so very appropriate for prayer.

It is really glorious, Emmy, to have the full peace of Jesus!! One really feels that in quite a different way when it has been disturbed!

Your happy Ebbo

Halle, July 7, 1907
My Ebbo,

I thought I could only write you a card today, but now I still have some time. Your sermon gives me a great deal! I am *very* happy that the Lord blesses you so richly. You express it very clearly that faith is *not* feeling but *deed*. I also find very fine what you say about the conceited disciples of the Lord:

"Out of your words you will be justified or condemned." I believe I must watch myself very much never to say more than what has really turned into deed. I mean quite especially that I never should speak about anything about which I do not yet have any certainty from the Lord, and perhaps repeat someone else's words about something that has not yet become action with me! Surely these words apply to this too?

Ebbo, your sermon makes me pray very much. Oh, if only *everything* I recognize would become deed! That is how it ought to be, and I hope it is like that. Only now have I rightly understood the parable of the two sons. I want to break with every sin with real resolve, but I am still so dreadfully imperfect. I notice this now again from your sermon! Pray that I may always look *only* to Him and not to myself or others. *Only* then will I come forward!

Above all, I am happy about your letter, that you are now again wholly happy in Jesus. I knew exactly what kind of struggles in prayer you had!

Loving you and praying very much for you, for your studies and everything,

Your faithful Emmy

Breslau, July 7, 1907

They praised God with jubilation! Acts 2:47

My Emmy,

I praise God with jubilation for His tremendous mercy, above all for your letter! The enclosed card also fits so wonderfully and refreshed me very much.

What made me happiest is that you write, "I am happy because you are again completely happy; I am too, in Jesus and in you!" O Emmy, that is just exactly how I feel! Your joy is my joy, and your pain is my pain.

Only now do I understand why in all the larger movements of awakening and evangelization they hold with stern firmness to having awakened men helped only by men, and women and girls only by women. Altogether in our whole movement this is a kind of rule in the care of souls. I shall be everywhere more strictly reserved than anyone else since I consider it my duty.

You know, we must not ask the world. There is maybe not one clear relationship in a thousand in the sense we mean it. Even among children of God we are *quite exceptionally* blessed. This is becoming more and more clear to me. My happiness seems to me like a deep, clear ocean that can never be exhausted.

Thanks to the Lord I now no longer have the slightest burden and am again strong in His joy. Whatever comes, I know I shall conquer, for Jesus and His Holy Spirit dwell with me. Therefore the little scenes between the others at home can in no way take me out of this peace. I rejoice that the Lord has brought it so far that I am even approached by both parents to see to it that there is peace, etc. You know, that of course this is very disagreeable for me as a son, and I keep as far from all conflicts as I possibly can. But the fact that I am now being called on is a witness *for Jesus,* whereas before I was always rebuked for bringing nothing but quarrel and strife by my Christianity.

Even now Papa sometimes gets rather annoyed about my attitude, but on the whole he is very nice to me. He himself always prays a great deal. As far as one can see, however, he does not find any strength in prayer. It is a sad kind of religion. O how I praise God for having given *victory* in Christ Jesus so that I know His joy, a life of happiness and strength!

My good parents again have no fault to find with our frequent writing. Mama only said, "But you can't exhaust the whole of theology, or of love either."

Let us be thankful when Jesus uncovers wounds and heals them. We do ask Him always to show us also those sins we are unaware of. I want to bear with thanks and praise even what is most painful if only I become purer and more usable for Jesus!

These days my thoughts, besides being with you, have also been a great deal with the students in Halle, and I have prayed for them a lot. A converted student has written to another one here, "Also through the circle here (German S.C.M.) one receives a powerful stimulus. The people are not, like those in Breslau, all of the same stamp dogmatically; on the contrary, the greatest variety of individuals and therefore of views rules here, yet at the same time the living Christ is in the *foreground*. In this way one learns. Compared with last semester, by the way, there will most likely be a setback. The enthusiasm coming from Arnold and Gerdtell has abated. This though is not the fault of the leader (Hans Wyszynski). I can only keep admiring him—a splendid person of 19 years, and 3 semesters! Even if it does not go on so stormily, yet we do expect a *deep* blessing."

You know, when I came to Halle, there was the utmost confusion in the German S.C.M. Remind me in August to tell you how, as an answer to *prayer*, God gave grace in victory

after victory to bring the Spirit of Jesus to rulership and to
drive back what is alien and unclear. We experienced wonderful, glorious things. But it wasn't I, nor Gerdtell either, nor
anyone else, but *the Lord* and *His Spirit.*

Anything that might have come from *us* must perish, the
faster the better. But let us pray, Emmy, that the Lord's work
may grow, may become deeper and clearer among the students
of Halle!

I have just been with Käthe's[17] brother, who was converted
about three years ago. My talks began his awakening. In the
YMCA he came completely to the Lord. A Bible class showed
him that he must put it into practice. Jesus be praised!! This
had an effect on Käthe, whom the Lord blessed in still a
different way, and she had an effect on Hermann, so that in
this way, as I implore, he will come to faith.

Emmy, gradually you too will be noticing how frightfully
wretched I myself am. But Jesus is my victory! Hallelujah to
eternity!

Ebbo

Breslau, July 14, 1907

Psalm 16:11!

My Emmy,

I am very shaken that you have already seen twenty to thirty
people meet death. I am completely with you in your feelings
about this! Last summer when I was in the tent mission, I too

---

[17] Käthe Treutler was engaged to Eberhard's older brother Hermann. She
came to the Cotswold Bruderhof as a widow and was our sister until her
death in Primavera, Paraguay, in 1956.

had a deeply shattering impression of how lost and far away from God men are! O Emmy, in Germany too there is so terribly much to do! Thousands die of thirst without a drop of living water! But certainly, still more outside. I yearn to be ready at last to use my whole strength in saving souls and in building up His Kingdom. But the one who leads us is *the Lord.*

Finney's talks are very incisive. Sharp self-examination is the best preparation for new blessings, assuming that we keep our eyes directed to *Jesus.* Writing things down is of course not necessary, but often advisable because it helps us to be accurate.

Your faithful Ebbo

Breslau, July 21, 1907

I shall pour out the spirit of grace and of prayer.

Zech. 12:10 [according to Luther's translation]
Unending joy shall be upon their heads! Isa. 35:10

My Emmy,

At this moment I have only the one wish, that you may be just exactly as happy as I am. The reason is not a new one. It is *Jesus* and *you!* What fullness of the power of grace and joy!

So go joyfully and courageously to Salzwedel as well! He will stand by us in the harder tasks. Matt. 10:19, 20. I am very glad that you do not want this restless rushing in the work. I believe the best orderliness is imparted by a quiet, joyful activity in the peace of Jesus.

Oh, how glorious it will be when we two live together and need not be guided by anyone but by our Lord alone! Thus here too, the life for Jesus and the life for you are just the same.

What shall we read now? Today we are as far as Acts 21, aren't we? Were you also struck by how free of all shyness was their fellowship in prayer? For example, Acts 21:5. The entire book of Acts is absolutely modern. In a thousand features it portrays the original Christian character of our awakening movement.

Couldn't you sometimes withdraw more to rest, in the afternoons and evenings? I believe it would be very good for body and soul. How much time do you actually have for Bible reading and prayer?

Eberhard

July 26, 1907. Breslau.
[Eberhard's birthday]

Following the Lamb!

Today of all days I praise Jesus continually because I have won *you*!

I have experienced much grace in the past year. Shortly before my last birthday I had become leader of the German S.C.M. in Halle, as you know. I regard outward successes and honors only as a dangerous and unpleasant by-product. But God has poured out eternal blessings upon me personally and upon the German S.C.M. The chief thing for me is to know that God has rescued souls from death and has accepted me as an instrument in this. How deeply He has made my unworthiness clear to me I want to show you later.

Through you I am happy and joyful through and through! Through you I have double and triple energy for my work! You are my deepest stimulus to follow the Lamb in holiness! You are the greatest strengthening for me to serve my Jesus alone, only for His glorification! And you are my most powerful and decisive encouragement to trust so utterly in Jesus for everything that the being-in-Him will give me certainty in regard to everything. Your wishes for me today I have brought before the Lord, sentence by sentence. They were absolutely from my heart.

My mood today is equally happy as it is serious. Happy in you and in Jesus, with whom I live in deep, glorious fellowship! Serious, thinking of the many defects in the year past, with the resolute certainty that Jesus shall conquer over me more than ever in the coming year. I have given up to Him my whole vanity and passionateness and have the blind trust in Him that He will protect me because He remains in me and I in Him. His blood and Cross are my saving and my joy.

In truth it is more and more that way; the more fully you and I put on Jesus (Romans 13:14) and are immersed in Him, the more fully and completely we shall be merged in each other.

God protect you,

Ebbo

Breslau, July 28, 1907

Not I, but Christ! Gal. 2:20

My Emmy,

I believe in God's working. Praise to Him from all my heart! May He make my life ever purer, ever more fruitful and

powerful. "I nothing, He all in all! How purely the blessing
will then pour forth! Let our voice resound jubilantly to praise
and honor Him alone!"

Ebbo

Galatians 2:20   Halle, July 30, 1907

My Ebbo,

At last I can again write to you in peace. Ebbo, I can be
very thankful to the Lord that Stappenbeck did not work out,
for it is terribly difficult to keep one's thoughts turned to Jesus
during constant rushing. With the Freybes it was often very
difficult. Right away on the first evening he began his conversation like this: "What is all this business in Halle about
baptism?" Then he started harping on sectarianism, and so on.
At first I quietly let him finish talking, and then said I believed
he had been wrongly informed. I then told about the great
blessing that has gone out from Herr von Gerdtell in Halle,
and finally came to the subject of baptism and unfortunately
had to admit that there have often been wrong actions by
children of God. Afterwards they told me that the Matron
showed them my letter, saying that I had probably come in
contact with the Fellowship. This gave me an opening to tell
them my present attitude to Jesus. Besides, he said, these
poeple always have to have some hobbyhorse. One time it is
conversion, another time baptism, Lord's Supper, or things of
the future, and the Cross is forgotten. He then asked me, "On
what do you base your salvation?" When I said, *"On Jesus,"*
he told me he had expected the answer, "On my conversion."

I find the quarrels here among the children of God frightfully sad. The same with the German S.C.M. Whatever would Jesus say? I shall be glad when I can tell you everything.

It will be glorious when we are able to pray together, also for all these things.

Your bride

Breslau, July 31, 1907

My Emmy,

Further, let us pray *very much* that God may give me authority and power to heal the damage in Halle completely. God can do wonders. His Spirit can make those who are His completely humble and bring them into harmony with one another. I feel, as it were, a task from the Lord, and feel the Scripture gives me this right, simply as a brother.

Ebbo

Breslau, August 2, 1907

Hallelujah! Honor and praise, glory and strength to God our Lord! Rev. 19:1

My Emmy,

I have just finished the Revelation with great joy and feel myself flooded through with a stream of strength from eternity. A wonderfully powerful, mighty book! And especially the Greek!

O Emmy, what an endlessly glorious thing is the power and peace of Jesus! Just in these days the Lord has humbled me very much. I realize how fully unworthy of Him and of you

I am in my wickedness. But today too the Lord again proved to me the power of Romans 5:20. I am saved, free, and happy through Jesus.

He makes all things new!! Rev. 21:5. Again I am blissful in Jesus' deepest happiness and peace about your fellowship. You really help your foolish Ebbo enormously to become more calm and sensible. And I know that I now have triumph and victory in Jesus and that this cannot be taken away from me so easily.

Your rich letters have refreshed and gladdened me. Yes, we shall have great blessing when we are together now!

Loving you in the Lord,

All your Ebbo

Halle, Aug. 6, 1907

Ephesians 3:13–21

My Ebbo,

After you had gone I was sad at first, but now I am happy in Jesus and in you again. May He bless your fellowship with Herr von Gerdtell and give you His Spirit and His strength so that He may be glorified during the conference days. Only tell me everything really in detail.

The letter from Fräulein von Nostiz moved me very much; I am sorry, however, that she does not see it! I would like best of all to send her a greeting some time, but don't know if it is right.

However, it has become clear to me through all this gossiping that it is not right in the Lord's eyes to discuss a child of God. Please also pray that I may not do it any more. Only to you will I tell everything, for you can tell me if you consider it wrong. I am sorry too for what I said about Frau Baehr. I consider it a great sin to judge her that way, since she has to give account to the Lord and also does this. I believe besides that she is more deeply rooted in God than I. It is fully clear to me how much I still am lacking, Ebbo! I thank you *very much* for telling me yesterday that it was not right.

Your faithful bride

Train from Halle to Berlin
August 6, 1907

Ephesians 3:20, 21

My Emmy,

Pray earnestly and joyfully that I may attain victory upon victory, just exactly the way it says in Eph. 3:20, 21!

To Him be glory!

To Him be glory!

To Him be glory!

Now and into eternity!

My Emmy, through everything and through me you are receiving very young, as a child of God, serious glimpses into the internal difficulties of our circle of believers. This could become dangerous and lead to faint-heartedness and discouragement about all believers, and so on. However, let it lead you *only* to becoming ever smaller yourself and to an ever deeper *Jesus only!*

In carrying, complete love for all believers,

Your Ebbo

Steglitz, Filandastr. 34
August 6, 1907

My Emmy,

Just think, before I had said a word about it, Ludwig von Gerdtell said he regretted very much that Frau Baehr was now placing baptism so very much in the foreground. To my question he said he had noticed this only from her letters. He then told me *something* about her and Fräulein von Nostiz. Von Gerdtell was very sad that it is that way and said he wished he could divert the brothers and sisters away from it to *Jesus* and the free conviction of conscience in Him. About the baptism of some in Halle he had rejoiced, he said, but it was terrible that the baptism propaganda this time too, as so often, was the death of the awakening. It was (he said) a ruin-bringing sin to let oneself be persuaded to be baptized unless one was *independently* convinced without any doubt that this was Jesus' clear will. He then said he had a better understanding with me than with the closest, truest friends he had among those baptized.

Now, come what may, Jesus is victorious!

In Jesus, our center,

Your Eberhard

Halle, Aug. 8, 1907

My Ebbo,

I was very happy with your letter and card. I am glad the Lord has answered our prayers like that and has given such a warm beginning to the conference. He will conquer, I am sure of that too!

What you write about Herr von Gerdtell was very interesting and enjoyable to me. I have a really colossal respect for him because he does not emphasize baptism, though he is baptized, but Jesus alone.

Your bride

Student Conference, Wernigerode
August 8, 1907

Like Christ! Eph. 5:25

My Emmy,

Just now, at 7:15, I have read Ephesians and prayed with joyful certainty for the conference, *you*, and our families.

Already on the train and then immediately at the station I was welcomed with terrific love and joy and soon realized that the agitation against us has not been able to get very far. It is so wonderful with what warm brotherliness our students meet each other. Somewhat more than 200 people have registered for the conference; the main public conference is to begin this evening. About half of them, perhaps one hundred students, are already here for the work conference. You have the programs. I was completely flabbergasted when the meeting did not nominate anyone at all besides me for first chairman and wasn't prepared for it in the least. But Jesus helped me through. Wyszynski spoke *well* about our Bible classes. He is *very* loving and loyal.

Now let us pray very faithfully and persistently that through this conference *many* students may come to clear conversion to Jesus alone! And even if it were only one, we would exult and jubilate. Let us pray further that Jesus conquer in the deliberations, that no conflict arise, and that all opposing or parallel currents be overcome. And third, let us pray that our brothers may take away with them from here powerful, deep strength for their work, that is, *the Holy Spirit!*

Your bridegroom

Halle, August 9, 1907

My only Ebbo,

Incidentally, Ebbo, yesterday I was in the so-called "Baptizers' Alliance Meeting" to show that I do not separate myself either from the baptized or from the child baptizers, but have fellowship with all the children of God. There is not supposed to be any one leader there anymore; instead the Holy Spirit alone is to lead. Perhaps because of this, rather long pauses arise frequently since no one feels urged.

Your faithful Emmy

Wernigerode, August 9, 1907
Afternoon

1 Cor. 15:57! To do His work! Eph. 2:10

Dear Emmy,

The report this morning, "Who was Jesus?" by Doktor Langmesser, was not worth much—biblical history with supposedly poetic-scholarly embellishments instead of conscience-cutting glorifying of Jesus.

I said something like this: "Jesus as Son of God demands submission and faith! Jesus as Son of Man in His power demands discipleship."

I spoke without *the calmness* that is simply necessary when we witness for Jesus, and therefore left out half of what I wanted to say; and that little bit I said in passionate agitation. I am quite bowed down and was quite despondent for a long time. But *He* has raised me up. I am thankful to Him for showing me over and over again *how* wretched and harmful I am so that *at last* He can build the pure and new upon the ruins of self. It was now all the clearer to me that I should not take part in the outing since I absolutely needed the quietness before Jesus. He holds me, and I hold Him.

All my weaknesses and faults notwithstanding, I continue to go forward, always looking to Jesus and knowing that He has created me for good works. Let us pray very much that Jesus may make something out of us, you know of course, to the praise of His glory!

Yes, we want to keep a tight rein on ourselves not to speak about children of God, or about people at all unless the Spirit commands it!

Your Eberhard

Halle, August 10, 1907

My Ebbo,

I am also very much humbled in these days; it is and becomes clearer and clearer to me that I am nothing and that as soon as I do not look clearly to Jesus I immediately sin again, and then I notice so plainly a rift between Jesus and myself.

Your faithful Emmy

Wernigerode, August 10, 1907

That only CHRIST may be proclaimed!

My Emmy,

If only *Christ* the *Crucified* and *Risen* is proclaimed! Spirit-preaching without proclamation of Christ is the most dangerous kind of enthusiasm (*Schwärmerei*). The Spirit is there only that He may glorify *Christ* and witness about *Him* and *His* words. See for example John 16:13, 14 (thus He does not speak about Himself!!); 15:26; 14:26.

May God's Spirit, this Spirit of Jesus Christ, bless and lead you all! That is what I pray for. Now God keep you.

Your faithful Ebbo

Halle, Aug. 11, 1907

My Ebbo,

You know, the Lord must make me still much freer for Him; we must pray very much for that. *Ach*, Ebbo, free of everything, only for Him! I seem so incapable to myself, especially in regard to Brumby. If only the children would come to Jesus!

Your faithful Emmy

Wernigerode, August 11, 1907

Each one like Jesus! Phil. 2:5

My bride,

When I have told you everything, you won't be surprised that I am writing to you only now. Yesterday morning, after a prayer by a former actor who was converted (years ago in Wernigerode) and is now studying theology, General von Viebahn spoke with mighty power on "Die, and come into being!" After him, Count Pückler, Doktor Langmesser, student Hommel, Stockhausen the engineer, and I spoke. All of us gave a clear witness. I had the victory of being able to tell in quietness and joyful vigor about my experiences of "Die, and come into being," thinking especially of my conversion, my separation from the world, and my time with the Salvation Army.

Today in private talks I had proof that Jesus blessed that morning very much. In the intermission I prayed with von Pathow (we now say "*du*" to each other) and Seemann.

At 2 o'clock we met for the outing; only two students spoke there about their inner struggles. May Jesus save them completely! The one was hindered by doubts, and so on, the other by his *ego*.

Yet all the noble and glorious and uplifting things are *nothing* to me in comparison with the Cross, in comparison with Jesus alone!

Your faithful Ebbo

Wernigerode, August 12, 1907
Afternoon

1 Cor. 15:57!

My Emmy,

My heart rejoices and exults in the victories of our Lord! Already now we can say in faith: souls are saved, brothers strengthened, and strongholds conquered!

Praise the Lord with me for His grace! God has equipped

Gerdtell mightily with His strength so that the students, in real student-fashion, have been convinced of the wretchedness of every kind of egotism and self-life and have been confronted by the God-given energy and power of men who are directed by Jesus Christ alone. I could tell you a great deal about how mightily the conference is in movement toward Jesus!

August 13

It was very good that I wrote that yesterday before the meeting. For in it we were very distressed. Gerdtell, von Tippelskirch, Still, and I stood absolutely together, and the Lord gave us strength for victory and for clear witness; thus we were able to leave the meeting with a clear conscience and then sit together in the *Gothenhaus* until nearly midnight. Our motion, put forward by me in the meeting, of quite a fundamental nature, was rejected by a majority of *one* vote, which we regarded as a very sad sign.

Your happy Ebbo

Breslau, Sept. 3, 1907

My Emmy,

How terribly much would I like to begin this letter really joyfully so as to comfort and encourage you. But I am still quite sad. In this frame of mind I see everything black as black can be—the baptism question, the German S.C.M. conflicts, the work for Gerdtell, our family difficulties, my exams, and everything.

But now about two hours after the beginning of this letter, I can finally tell you I am again happy and calm in Jesus, if not so joyful and cheerful that I could laugh a great deal.

On the basis of God's Word I have accepted His forgiveness and help and give Him everything, completely. *The Word of the Lord* here again is the sole source of strength for me, for faith and obedience. I ask Him to make me really, really simple, utterly simple, in regard to His Word. I need that very much, and I *want* it. The words of 1 Peter 1:24 and 25 have just become important to me, surely from the Lord. If we stand completely in the *Word*, our happiness and our victory will never be a passing one but will remain for eternity.

I can't disregard Gal. 3:25, 27. I feel that I am facing tremendous decisions, and I shall simply and definitely obey God as soon as I have certainty.

But I trust Jesus. Follow the Lamb wherever He goes!

Your bridegroom

Breslau, Sept. 4, 1907

2 Peter 3:14, 15

My bride,

This hour of prayer and dedication has brought me a serious, momentous decision which will give our life a sharply defined direction, laden with suffering.

Emmy, my brave, faithful bride, you are of course the first person to whom I am telling this, that today I have been convinced by God, in quietness and sober biblical certainty, that baptism of believers alone is justified. Taking Gal. 3:26, 27 as a starting point, I felt clearly in persevering reflection with Jesus, in simple, truthful prayer, that Scripture knows only one baptism, that of those who have become believers. Since to me the Bible is the revelation of God and His will, fully adequate in itself and incapable of being added to, it reveals to me the will of my God and unmasks the baptism of unbelieving (or more correctly, not-believing) infants as not coming from the Holy Spirit.

I therefore regard myself as unbaptized, and hereby declare war on the existing Church system.

Until Sunday I shall find out pretty well what stand scholarship takes on this question, still wait a while until you express your opinion, and then inform our parents on both sides. It is of course my wish to be baptized as soon as possible and to leave the established Church. You will help me, however, by remaining completely calm and doing *nothing hasty*.

Of course, the position you take on this question, my only life companion, is of most tremendous significance for me. You were in fact already clearer than I. But I beg you urgently to let my decision be your incentive *only* to test this biblical question still more carefully and thoroughly than before and to let Scripture *alone* decide.

I will be very glad to wait for you for as long as my conscience at all allows. Should you, contrary to all expectation, be convinced that "infant baptism" is willed by God, I of course don't need to say that our complete fellowship will in no way be affected by this, however much I should like us to have the same views on this point too.

Let us not say anything to *anybody* to begin with. You must on no account hint anything of it to anybody before I myself have come out with it. I shall still wait a short time so as to see clearly in all directions and to allow you time.

What will happen then the Lord knows. And that is sufficient. I know only one thing, that Matt. 19:29 is gloriously true and that Jesus will lead us excellently.

I ask of you, my Emmy, the same holy peacefulness that I am allowed to have through Jesus, so that no worry about the future may oppress you, for He cares for you. Trust joyfully in Jesus! The victory is yours!

I cannot say how thankful and happy I am that Jesus has given you to me, Emmy! Now that I have YOU, it will be so easy when everyone gives me up and misunderstands me. But let us *pray* that our dear ones may be brought by everything closer to Jesus, not to the Enemy! We will cause them great pain. That is hard, very hard, but perhaps their salvation. Oh, if I only had you here to talk everything over!!!

Let us write to each other daily in these important days. Write to me very fully about everything you think and feel. Now I have much strength from the Lord again.

From your Ebbo

The Lamb We Follow[18]

The Lamb we follow! Brothers, sisters,
Now nevermore shall we have fear.
His way shall lead us onward surely,
E'en though the furious foe we hear.

[18] As adapted and set to music by Marlys Swinger, 1970.

The Lamb we follow! Such deep oneness!
To put our trust in Him alone,
To follow faithfully His pureness,
Eternally to be His own!

The Lamb we follow! Such great power!
Guided by Him at every step!
Through deepest pain, through greatest efforts
Shall we be carried by His strength.

The Lamb we follow! Deeply joyful,
On His way going hand in hand,
In exultation as in sorrow
Faithfully at His side to stand!

The Lamb we follow! Quiet, peaceful,
Trusting in Him, serene and still,
In word and song forever praising,
While for Him living, by His will!

The Lamb we follow! What blest hoping
In coming dawn of glorious Day!
For vanished now is what oppressed us—
Evermore we sing His praise!

E.A. Sept. 4, 1907

Breslau, Sept. 5, 1907

Jerem. 1:6–9!

My Emmy,

Warmest thanks for your telegram and the dear letter. The
Lord has taken all the agitation and pain of separation away

from me and made me quiet and joyful. I am full of happiness when I think of you. How gloriously we wandered the sunny heights with Jesus. Oh, what fullness of the most marvelous memories is hidden in the past month. Our Jesus has again allowed us to look so truly into the depths of His tender love.

Let us answer Him with complete love, with total, joyful obedience of faith.

I felt rather bad about it that right away in your first days in Brumby I burdened you so heavily with things like baptism and German S.C.M. Yet both of us want it no other way; we want always to know, feel, and carry everything together right away.

It is remarkable that not only Loofs and Beyschlag, but also Feine, Kattenbusch, and Drew state that infant baptism cannot be shown to be biblical, and all of them lean to the view that in apostolic times the only ones who were baptized were those who accepted Jesus as Messiah and Lord and wished to become part of the original Christian Church (*Gemeinde*). Actually all of them give recognition only to baptism of the converted, as an act of submission to Christ and an act of acceptance into the Church. I shall write more about this to you tomorrow since it occupies me very much.

I now doubt very much whether I shall finish with my checking as soon as I thought yesterday. I am now considering particularly the command to baptize in Matthew 28. I shall not make my conviction known until it is clarified from every angle.

To be able to go through life with you is joy to me however hard the way may be. Yet I know quite clearly that even we two, or we especially, are nothing without *Jesus. Him* we praise and honor, to *Him* we live, through *Him* we are so happy, through *Him* we love each other so completely, and in *Him* we are victorious over everything.

From tomorrow on I simply must be more brief. If only I knew soon what is going to happen about the exam.

Loving you in Jesus,

Your Ebbo

1 John 5:3, 4!   Breslau, Sept. 6, 1907

My Emmy,

I am so endlessly peaceful and happy in my Savior.

We will now soon have six months of our engagement time, a time of untold happiness, behind us. Let us not complain, Emmy, if the second six months seems likely to begin with the most difficult family struggles. My conviction regarding baptism is so clear to me after very sober reflection that I consider a change of mind practically out of the question.

I feel as though scales have fallen from my eyes. I do not find a single passage that proves the possibility of infant baptism. But I do see quite a number of distinct scriptural passages presupposing actual conversion to Christ before baptism, in part specifically when defining baptism. Accordingly, no baptism exists except that which takes place upon full acceptance of Christ (Gal. 3:26, 27), upon linking the cleansed conscience to God (1 Peter 3:21), therefore upon dying to Christ (Col. 2:11, 12; Rom. 6:2–4).

The passages about circumcision (Rom. 4:11; Col. 2:11) which I formerly interpreted differently I now understand to mean that earlier in the Old Covenant, Abraham's *natural* descendants received circumcision as his blessing, the seal of his faith (soon after birth). In the New Covenant, however, *only those* who follow Abraham in *personal faith* are "children of Abraham." (Romans 4:12, 16, 17) In accordance with this, only those who have become believers can receive the circumcision of the New Covenant, that is, baptism with water, and they do this as young children in Christ, that is, immediately after their conversion.

Nor is Matthew 28:18–20 any proof to me against baptism of believers. The explanation of the Greek would be too lengthy here to show that in my opinion the passage should be understood and translated as follows: Make disciples of (bring to faith) all nations, and in doing so baptize them and teach them to keep everything. Nothing is said about the order of events, but only that the baptizing and teaching are alongside bringing people to faith and subordinate to it. It is simply part of it as a self-evident supplement.

The passage in my opinion does not *prove* anything. At the very most this one thing, that baptism belongs to *making disciples* and cannot be separated from that.

I am still thinking a great deal about this passage. But enough about that. I only wanted to give you a glimpse into my thoughts. What is decisive for me is not the books I am reading now by theologians inside and outside the Church, but the words of the Spirit in the Bible.

To you I will also write today and ask you to test the question with calm, careful, all-round consideration and not to take a definite inner stand on it until God's will is really clear to you.

Your bridegroom

Breslau, Sept. 7, 1907

My Emmy,

After having studied the baptism question this morning and finding my conviction confirmed over and over, I need very much to relax a little in a short letter to you.

Oh, it is so important that everything, everything, becomes thoroughly penetrated by Christ and that His name and word do not sound strange in connection with anything we do!

We want to remain completely *in Him*.

Papa said yesterday, after a very decided witness by me, that he did not have this decisiveness, that perhaps this came about because he had it too good in life. Let us pray very much for him. I am constantly with you in prayer. Jesus protects and strengthens you. May He give you a Sunday full of sunshine.

Forever your Ebbo

Just a few things quickly about your letter that just arrived and that moved and shook me *most deeply*.

1) I shall wait another week then, without saying a word to any of our parents.

2) More tomorrow about established Church and exams. I want to be very prudent and careful.

3) I *pray* for your recognition, but I do not want to force it from God. It comes from God that we are not together now so that each can reflect and decide independently.

4) *Please* do not press the Lord, but trust in Him quietly and firmly. I want to do just the same.

Breslau, August 8, 1907[19]

Praise the Lord!

My Emmy,

Leaving the established Church is, or at least seems to me, entirely a matter of truthfulness since I consider its system untruthful through and through. Still, since this question is not primarily a biblical one, I can perhaps wait longer with it than with baptism, although I will most likely not change my view.

It is *very well* possible, of course, that our Lord will guide the matter much more gently than our fearful hearts think. For His name is Wonderful, Counselor! However, we do not have a promise for outward peace, but for the sword.

If you feel my coming is necessary because of the difficulty of communicating by letter on such momentous questions as leaving the established Church, you need only call, and I will be there.

Your faithful bridegroom

Breslau, Sept. 8, 1907

1 John 5:3, 4

My dear Ludwig! [von Gerdtell]

The past week is one of great and consequential significance for me.

It is as if scales had fallen from my eyes to realize that

[19] Probably Sept. 8, letter number 93 following number 92 above.

Scripture witnesses to *that* baptism, and that baptism only, which is carried out on believers.

You know to a large extent what grave consequences for me will result from this, consequences that will cast my entire life into a sharply defined path.

A number of very serious questions are now forced upon me, in which I ask for your friendly help.

1) How and when I can step out of the established Church, whose lying system (as I see things at the moment) I cannot approve by silence.

2) Whether I can then continue working toward my first exam in theology, or whether I shouldn't rather switch over immediately to the study of philosophy.

3) Whether I can yield in any way to the requests and threats from my parents and parents-in-law that are to be expected on the point of the timing of my baptism.

4) Whether I should turn right away to a missionary society or go by what you have said and first take one exam quickly and then immediately place myself at the disposal of your work.

In order to allow myself and my dear bride time to gain a position that is clarified on all sides as much as possible, I shall still remain silent about everything for a week; so only my bride and you are informed, which you will bear conscientiously in mind.

I now have this *great* favor to ask of you, that you consider before the Lord whether you can visit me here one day this week. Of course you could not stay at our house; instead we would have to meet at the railway station. Unfortunately, for several reasons, I consider the reverse possibility that I might go to you in Steglitz *completely out of the question* for these weeks. You will understand how much a thorough-going personal talk would mean to me, especially since there are still other questions to discuss besides those I have mentioned.

Please greet your dear wife very warmly from me. I hope she is better again. I would be glad to hear how she is. My dear, brave bride is a great support to me in this time. We both know that we can rely completely on Jesus. Faithfully united in Him and looking forward very much to you,

Your friend,
Eberhard Arnold

P.S. Please send me a telegram, or write by return mail if possible.

Breslau, Sept. 9, 1907

"Love as if you were all heart!
Witness as if you were steel and brass!
And you will conquer on all sides."

Bernhard Kühn

My sunshine,

You shall have just a short sign of life and love from me today.

Since an hour of blessing this morning, I am again more calm and joyful in Him and in you. I want always to keep in mind that the chief thing after all is that our souls, prayers, and thoughts remain completely one even when we are quite far apart.

In my studies of the baptism and Church questions I am being most deeply blessed by God.

Now that I have a sharper eye for religious lying among men, it is the *Cross* that is becoming ever greater for me, the *Cross* upon which Jesus hung, rejected and condemned by those who were perhaps the most religious and pious people of all times. And in submitting to this culminating sin on the part of unregenerate religiosity *He atoned for it* so that all who want it are fully forgiven. If we understand *the Cross* in its realness and clearness, the religious lie of the nations with their "formal" Christianity stands unmasked as rebellious, selfish life and hostility to God. *Through the Cross* we recognize the reality of every sin, including the sin that is covered up with religious disguise. And at the same time we are struck with ever new astonishment at the unbelievable love of God and Jesus which reverses this greatest wickedness of (pious!) mankind and turns it to the full redemption of all who believe. And third, we see how the seemingly highest and ultimate triumph of enmity over truth becomes the actual, consummated victory of truth over everything.

As a second train of thought, I feel it important that God wills us to be fully redeemed from all earthly restrictions of existence and success so that, like Abraham, we go the way shown us by the Word of God although we do not see it.

If we put a complete stop to placing our trust in anything that originates on earth, if we live completely in the heavenly, that is, if we simply follow the Word of the Lord, we shall lie utterly and safely in the arms of God! Oh what bliss to take account of nothing except Him!

My new position is growing more and more certain. My refuge is the *Word*. Thinking can always lead astray since circumstances have become enormously confused. But when I look at *Scripture* in its *entirety* and in *separate* passages, when I allow *the Spirit* of the Old Testament and above all of the New Testament to work on me and then in addition to this take the *specific* utterances, it becomes ever clearer and surer to me that Jesus *never* baptized unconverted masses or wanted to have them Christianized formally, that is, hypocritically. No; *He* and the apostles wanted *only* total conversions of individual persons, wanted them to band together, separate from the world in every respect. The documentation of this in Scripture can easily be found in abundance.

The historical rise of the Church of the masses confirms the fact that its origin was not from the Holy Spirit, who dwells only in people who are reborn.

Oh, how much I would prefer to tell you in person of the many thoughts that have been rushing in on me *from God*, as I definitely believe.

But we know that our separation in space is from the Lord too. And you understand me this way as well, and will do so more and more. And you also see it this way, that I want only the one thing for you and for me, that we both become filled completely by the Spirit of Jesus Christ, who is a Spirit of absolute truth. Please write to me in fullest detail all doubts and wishes, questions and thoughts. I need them now more than ever.

Your faithful Ebbo

Breslau, September 10, 1907

They who looked upon Him became radiant of countenance, *beamed with joy,* and their countenance never had to grow pale. Psalm 34:5

My Emmy,

It gave me great joy to look up and translate the above words for you. The first expression is translated twice. "Became radiant of countenance" stems from the Kautzsch Bible. The second expression, the better in my opinion, I got from the lexicon.

Dear Emmy, I want to write very deeply on your heart so that from there it will always shine forth: *"They who look upon Him beam with joy!"*

Notice too that this verse is in our engagement Psalm! We will praise the Lord *at all times*; His praise shall *evermore* be upon our lips.

You see, my bride, how much it concerns me that you are too quiet and serious in Brumby. O Emmy, do not look at the fact that I am not with you fully in person; or that you have no fellowship; do not look at what baptism may perhaps bring us, or at the looks and words of the good pastor. Instead *look upon the Lord* and you will *beam* with joy!

But by looking in trust at Jesus we are nevertheless freed from all that oppresses and drags down. Up with your eyes to the sunny heights, up into the heavenly places where Jesus is and where the prayers of your Ebbo are too, *up to Jesus,* and the joyful victory is yours.

You know that I say all this just as much to myself, and I shall be endlessly comforted, refreshed, and gladdened by these heights of mercy and love. For your letters, both of which I received this morning, I thank you most warmly.

It is good that you are able to distinguish between a pious atmosphere and true Christianity. Anyone who has no inkling of living according to the Word of God is unreborn and lost in spite of the most pious religiosity (1 John 5:3; 4:6; 2:3–5; 2 John 9; Gospel of John 14:21, 23; 8:47; and many other passages, though these are probably the clearest). Whoever does not confess the Lord in words, will not be recognized by Jesus with *one* word either (Matt. 10:32, 33). His command in this connection, verse 27, stands and remains unqualified for all who have Him.

I thank the Lord from my heart for your witness, which He has brought about! The more fully you follow Him only, the more radiant will be your happiness.

I am *very* glad that you are testing the baptism question quietly and without haste, my Emmy; it does not surprise me at all. Until next Sunday, then, let neither of us say anything to anybody. If the Lord wishes it for further clarification, we will also wait still longer though I am certainly not much in favor of this at the moment. What you write about thinking it over without being influenced is very important. Quite disregarding all the people who are for and against, we must ask *Scripture*, our only authority, without tolerating any supplementation, the smallest addition, or the smallest subtraction. Jesus gave such sharp warning against the Pharisees because they made supplements and additions to Scripture and watered down and spiritualized the meaning of the words; and against Herod because he was a halfling—he tried to be partly obedient, partly disobedient.

It is clear that you must inform Herr and Frau Pastor Freybe as soon as your conviction is so beyond question that you write it to your parents.

Your faithful Ebbo

Breslau, Sept. 11, 1907

Peace like a stream of water! Isaiah 48:18

My Emmy,

It is really true: The more deeply, honestly, and obediently we search the commands of the Lord, seeking to listen to them as closely as possible, the more gloriously will His peace grow in our hearts.

I am so happy that this experience that is filling me with bliss right now is yours too, as I hear from you today, "He is so close to me as He has hardly ever been, and I rely on Him completely." My Emmy, I am very thankful to the Lord for revealing to us both at the same time the important truths of baptism of believers and Gemeinde of believers, truths which so strongly disclose the holiness of God.

Gerdtell's letter is so full of genuine good sense and loving concern that you will be very glad about it. I answered him immediately and gave him some insight into how *the Lord* is leading us.

Further, I asked him to be here on Friday or Saturday, and I now definitely expect him.

I shall then immediately write you the outcome of our talk and ask you on no account to say anything to anyone unless truthfulness demands it. I assume, naturally, that you have written nothing to Frau Baehr or Else. As soon as we see *fully* clearly in *everything*, not before, we shall write *together* to our parents and offer them a personal talk in October. To the "Pastors" [the Hachtmanns] I would say nothing before the trip to the actual baptism except as I wrote above.

Warmest thanks for your letter!

Your faithful Ebbo
Jesus!

Breslau, Sept. 13, 1907

1 Cor. 4:20. The Kingdom of God stands in *power*!

My Emmy,

The Kingdom of God stands not in words, not in feelings, not in thoughts, but in *power*.

I want to make an effort to make your engagement time more inwardly quiet in the future, and I shall have the strength for this from the Lord.

For your last letter of September 10—I am just about to thank you, and here comes your letter of the 12th today. I am so very happy that the Lord is your strength and that He *commands* me and you to be courageous and joyful. This saying and your whole letter refreshes and gladdens me most deeply. You will notice from the first pages that I was somewhat or very much downcast. But now I am really confident and joyful. Your letter is a powerful, deep joy to me. I enjoy so much thinking of the marvelous afternoon when we strolled along the narrow field paths in splendid sunshine like today's and were so happy in Jesus; of how we told Him this in prayer under the tree, and then had such a wonderful undisturbed time together for coffee, with the peaceful orchard and the quiet village before us and the pastoral scene behind us; of how we went back along the path, picking flowers for little Gustav[20] as we went and talking together and wishing our dear ones just as great a happiness if possible. Yet one thing is never over, and that is that we go hand in hand through life and eternity and that for us there will always be sunshine because Jesus is our Sun.

Actually the difficult thing will not be that *we* are forsaken and threatened, but that we will have to see ourselves as the cause of terrible pain for people who are so very dear to us, to whom of all people we owe the most, apart from what we have from one another. I believe this will spur us on very much to deeper love for all the people who resist. One thing we will also hold to firmly: also for our dear ones, the way of complete obedience of faith *must* be the best thing we can give them though all appearances may be against it. Truth always has a saving and healing effect—on the upright. We want to pray all the more for our loved ones and be more loving than ever.

Gerdtell was extremely loving and sensible yesterday. He asked me very much never to place baptism in the foreground but simply to proclaim *Christ* and to include baptism with that *silently* as the natural consequence.

1) On Monday I shall inform our parents briefly (letter in

[20] Emmy's youngest brother who died very young.

Halle Tuesday morning) of my conviction, according to which I must first be baptized as a believer, since child baptism is in opposition to the biblical meaning and Word and is no baptism; second, I must withdraw from the established Church since I consider it dishonest through and through and contrary to the spirit of the Bible, and third, I consider my ideal to be Church communities (*Gemeinden*) of believing, baptized children of God, with Church discipline and the Lord's Supper.

2) I shall yield to our parents on the matter of timing to the extent that they are honestly willing to give me the opportunity to hear counter arguments and to reply; in this my only criterion is Scripture, by which I shall gladly allow myself to be refuted. I shall then write immediately to Mascher [a preacher] in Steglitz and will presumably be able to be baptized at the end of September or the beginning of October.

3) I shall personally request the General Superintendent (a dreadful word) or Bishop to permit me to take the first exam in spite of my withdrawal from the established Church, something that actually is not possible. If he *does not* allow me to do this, I will have done my duty and will switch over to philosophy with a clear conscience. So this is completely in God's hand.

4) I am not able to postpone leaving the established Church any more than I can postpone the actual baptism. For I regard the Church's lying system as Satan's most dangerous weapon and the most treacherous foe of apostolic Christianity. Of course I do not fail to recognize the uprightness of many Churchmen and the fact that they are blessed children of God, who are used by the system to disguise its shamefulness.

5) I shall seek to get to know the German Baptist Churches

since they have very biblical principles and shall perhaps, even if not very probably, join them later, since their confession (and to a lesser extent their life) is very much in keeping with my ideal.

6) I shall be employed in Gerdtell's work immediately after my first exam (theology or Doctor of Philosophy).

I would be glad to avoid withdrawing from the Church and shall also think it over very much these days. But as often as I ask my conscience and the Bible, my recognition leaves me no other course. You of course will not do this since you are not convinced. I shall not send you the book about the history of the struggle between the established Churches and the true Church (*Gemeinde*) until I can do without it, perhaps on Monday. On the other hand you will receive the one about *Gemeinde* and baptism today. My markings, etc., surely won't bother you.

I was out for a walk with Gerdtell yesterday, and by the banks of a peaceful stream we prayed and talked over these questions. He also remembered you very nicely, though I told him very little or hardly anything about us two. You know how reluctant I am to do this because nobody understands it. He said we should also move to Marburg later so that we and our wives could become really intimate friends. He had supper with me at home and greeted Papa in a very friendly and polite way.

That you, my dear, have already told our secret to Else and through her, to Frau Baehr! It is really tremendously difficult to keep complete silence. I fear so very much that the story will now get around before Monday. For that moves fast as lightning. *I hope* Frau Baehr knows that she must be completely quiet about it. Have you written this to her once more? Dear Emmy, I believe you must learn still better to keep silence.

True, I do find it very understandable and very obvious in this case, but I would consider it *much* better if Else too had been taken by surprise. That would in my opinion have been much easier for her. I hope I am mistaken in this.

Yes, Frau Baehr is right. We must rejoice with pure joy that we are considered worthy to suffer for Him, our King.

Now Jesus protect you!

His strength is strong!

His peace is deep!

And His blood is invincible!

"I have commanded you to be courageous and joyful."

The prayers of your Ebbo surround you like a wall. And yours are like sunshine to him.

Your faithful Ebbo

Breslau, Sept. 15, 1907

Psalm 34:8, 9

My Emmy,

I am using this Sunday above all for a time of quiet and for prayer. I always become very quiet and sure when I open out God's Word before Him and pray for you and myself. Our course can be certain only if it is based on God's *Word* (Psalm 119:133, 160, 104, and 6). So it is impossible for me to doubt the truth of our recognition. The more I speak with the Lord about the thoughts of His Word, the firmer, surer, and more joyful I become in our new position. Yes, I feel and am aware that through this I am for the first time becoming a whole, complete character. For an important part of the person of Jesus was His truthfulness in holy ruthlessness in protesting against all human forms of religion and all hypocrisy and half-heartedness. We want the whole Christ. And the whole Christ shall have us whole.

Can we still feel worries, still feel anxiety when we see how He leads us forward by His Word with a sure hand? Must we not, just when we take steps of obedience, lay claim to the promises of the same Word? Are we not literally carried by words such as Ps. 34:8 or John 16:33 and many others? Yes, let us remain confident and joyful! Let us praise Him with jubilation for being allowed to follow Him! Already in earlier struggles I learned by experience that the harder the temptations for the sake of the Word, the deeper and more glorious becomes the peace in one's heart. Therefore we want to pray this time too and look to the Lord, and then we shall *beam*.

I shall wait on leading from the Lord as to whether I should inform my dear parents here on Monday evening or Tuesday morning—as considerately as possible.

For myself I have no worries about anything. On the contrary, the struggle for Jesus has always been joy and delight to me, and the more so the hotter it gets.

Isn't their sadness and being upset about us like a drop compared with the ocean of unhappiness when they endure torments of despair in eternity far from God? Isn't the pain of God and Jesus (Golgotha!) millions of times greater and holier than their indignation over the obedience of truth that causes it? Therefore let us *pray*, *pray*, and again *pray* that they may be saved from the Hell of being far from God, which

is making them so unhappy. It is not we who cause their unhappiness, but their alienation from God, their error, against
which we are fighting. The more obedient and faithful we are,
the more we shall serve toward their salvation.

My Emmy, surely you will remain steadfast and joyful?
Write to me very often. I pray and believe for you. He is your
peace.

Your Ebbo

Breslau, Sept. 16, 1907

1 Cor. 1:12–18

My Emmy,

Your letters of Saturday gave me tremendous joy and are of
the highest value for me. The chief thing for you will perhaps
be that through this I have come away for good from my plan
to become a Baptist; I believe I can say this already now. I
have been led this way by the true image of the Church,
which is actually present, which we must strive for, and which
we can attain (Matt. 18:15–18; 16:18; Acts 2:41–47—only
those who were *saved* did *the Lord* add to the *Church*—
1 Cor. 1:2; 2 Cor. 1:1; Gal. 1:2, and so on).

There are in the New Testament:

1) *Congregations or Churches (Gemeinden)—local,* exclusive alliances of the believers in a place or in a house (Romans
16:5; 1 Cor. 16:19; and so on).

2) *The Church of a town or place, (Die Gemeinde einer
Stadt oder eines Ortes)*: the complete unit of all believers
living there (1 Cor. 1:2, etc.).

3) *The Church* (*Die Gemeinde*): meaning all believers of all lands and all times (Eph. 1:22, 23).

All these *Gemeinden*, Churches, apart from (3) for the moment, had without doubt none but believing, baptized members.

But you are quite right. Today one cannot make baptism a condition, *for it is not recognized by each one as the command of Jesus.* It will surely once again become so *clear* that everyone who surrenders to Jesus obediently in faith will have to be baptized. But it *is* not this way as yet. For this reason the Baptist Church comes in fact into the category of 1 Cor. 1:12, 13; 3:4. The name "Baptists," by the way, has been more or less forced on the Churches as a mocking name. But their *principle* is that of a separatist party (sect). We want to stress only one thing in time and Eternity: *Jesus Christ! Jesus only! He as Lord and God whatever the consequences!* Baptism belongs to this for the individual, but only after the corresponding surrender.

I think my present draft of the letter to our parents will find your approval. This unity of the whole Church (with baptism) as in apostolic times will come for certain, *at the latest* through the persecutions of the last days of the world.

I thank you very, very much for having helped me in such a clear and decisive way in this important question. I am so happy that you tell me everything and very specially that you tell it to me so plainly.

I don't believe it is overhasty, my Emmy, if we come out with it now. On the contrary, openness demands it, for we are really completely clear now.

About when your baptism should take place I can only advise you as follows:

1) Do nothing that could be interpreted as deceitfulness.

2) Do not let yourself be persuaded to make any kind of promise.

3) Hold firm to the duty of taking the step as soon as possible.

Everything else will result from the leading of the Lord. For the present I shall do nothing toward your baptism. We want never to forget that during your engagement you are always completely subordinated to your parents and responsible to them. Of course you know perfectly well that I never mean this against Jesus.

In regard to the Hachtmanns you are absolutely right. I only thought it was good to know their attitude since in case of need I would have suggested placing a classified advertisement about you as a decidedly Christian lady who speaks French well and is musical. Perhaps more about this soon.

It is certainly very right that you wish me also to tell you *everything* about the struggles that are to be expected. I would have been glad to avoid doing this or to soften it so as not to make it too hard for you. But that would again have been untruthful. I shall report to you the whole truth, and you do the same for me. I pray that it may turn out easier than we think. 1 Cor. 10:13 is glorious. For myself I have no fear *at all*, only for you. I have deepest, most joyful peace. Yes, let us write every day this week, or else we will worry after all about each other. I thank you very warmly for what you tell me about your childhood! Do that really often.

Your Ebbo

Breslau, Sept. 17, 1907
[Tuesday]

1 Cor. 13:4–7

My Emmy,

Just think, I haven't said anything yet, and am very sad about it. It came like this: this morning I thought I wouldn't spoil Betty's birthday dinner by scenes in the family. After dinner Papa was not really available since his time was very full until about 7 o'clock, when he had to go to a banquet. I accompanied him so that I could tell him. However, when he was so terribly loving to me, as he has been all the time these last days, and poured his heart out to me about how God has led him through joys and disappointments, difficult things and marvelous things, I didn't find the courage to tell him that I would have to lay a new burden upon him, even though the opportunity was given me. You know, it is much, much more difficult for me to reply to such love and kindness with things which must be felt as blows than if for example I were sharply attacked for Jesus' sake. But I believe that this very thing comes from the Lord—that just in these days I feel how very, very deserving of love our dear ones are, so that my heart bleeds when I have to hurt them. But I must do it, for anything that suppresses the truth out of softness is never at any time the love that comes from God (1 Cor. 13:6). I therefore feel my silence as flabbiness and lack of courage, lack of *strength* FROM GOD, and thus had to humble myself very much before Him. However, since I absolutely must speak with Papa *before* speaking with Mama and since he is giving exams actually the *whole* day tomorrow from 8 o'clock on,

I will have to speak to him at about 7:30 a.m. tomorrow, probably while accompanying him. I am sure that tomorrow I shall have the strength for a clear witness through *Jesus*, His *Word*, His *Blood*, and His *Spirit*. I will not contest that my failure today may possibly be willed by the Lord so that I might still really show love and above all be completely, completely penetrated by my own powerlessness. I now throw myself on Him alone and trust in Him for the victory! You will understand my poem.

Your letters to me and Betty made me very happy.

How are you? We must now take particular care of our health. I am somewhat weary and tired out, otherwise well and cheerful. I shall write to you before noon tomorrow so that you will get the letter early. God protect you.

Your Eberhard

Out of Weakness, Strength!

O Lord, Thou hast proved once more
How poor I am and without strength.
So may Thy blood alone be praised—
Accept me as poor and weak as I am!
Yes, Lord, Thou hast broken in me once more
All building on my own strength;
I will never boast of this again;
For human strength brings only misery.
So let me trust in Thee alone,
Thou, King Jesus, Prince of Peace!
And I shall see victory after victory

For Thou shalt be victorious.
So I will stride forward, rejoicing.
Victory is mine in eternity.
Thou wilt lead me firmly through everything.
Where *Thou* art, there is no more a sorrowful heart.

Amen.

Sept. 17, 1907

In the following letter from Emmy to Eberhard's mother, the words in parentheses are those suggested by Eberhard for insertion.

Brumby, Sept. 17, 1907

Can I write the letter like this? If not, please answer immediately, as I will send it off as it is on Thursday.

My beloved Mother!

For your birthday I wish to send you the very warmest wishes for happiness and blessing to tell you that I always think of you, and very specially on your birthday, in warm love and respect, particularly in prayer. I hope you can use the little tablecloth. (Could you also express your joy that Mama's health is much better? She has never had any more pains.)

Through Ebbo you will know now that through Scripture we both have come to the decision to have ourselves baptized, a decision which may have difficult consequences. I am unable to consider infant baptism to be baptism as the Bible shows it and therefore must have myself baptized. You will surely feel this step as something very painful, yet we cannot do differently; our Christ-engrafted conscience urges us to do it.

Today I received a letter from my parents in Halle telling me that our dear father will not pass through Halle now after all, about which they and I are extremely sorry. It would be so nice if the two fathers could get to know each other since they would certainly get along very well together. Everyone had looked forward so much to Papa's visit. I suppose it is hardly possible that you might come to Halle? I would like so terribly much to see you again to speak with you in person about the many questions that are now moving us so very much. But of course Ebbo is there, and he can explain everything to you.

I am getting along quite well here. Today I am alone with the children since their parents are out of town. We are having very uncomfortably wet autumn weather, so I am sitting upstairs with them. I hope you are having nice weather in Breslau.

(Could you tell a bit more? Perhaps about the children or about what your duties are. The more you tell about yourself the more joy it gives Mama.)

Please do greet dear Father and Eberhard's brother and sisters very warmly. To you once more a very hearty greeting on your birthday,

from your loving and thankful daughter Emmy

To Emmy from her father

Halle, Sept. 17, 1907

My dear beloved child!

I have just written to Ebbo. Now it is your turn. I shall

write to you quite briefly. I hope to speak with you personally soon.

You can well imagine that your letters, which found us quite unprepared, have made us very sad. Mama, who was already very well, has been very unwell again since this morning. So hard did the news contained in your letters hit her.

You know, my beloved Emmy, that I discuss such religious questions only with reluctance. Each one must get along for himself as best he can.

In faithful warm love,

Your father

Breslau, Sept. 18, 1907

In all these things we shall overcome greatly!

My Emmy,

Only fifteen minutes are left for me until 11:30, and I hope I will then still be allowed to go off at night on my bicycle.

This noon came Papa's [Emmy's father's] letter assuring me very lovingly that our personal relationship of course remained as before. On the other hand he required:

1) the first exam in theology.
2) that we write to each other only twice a week.
3) that you wait one year with baptism.
4) that we not see each other for one year.

You will see what my attitude is to 1), 2), and 4) from the enclosed letter, which I can't possibly copy for you today. Let us be courageous and trust in Jesus. Just think, when Hannah came to me very nicely before coffee time and asked what was going on, I acted so queerly, and when she asked whether perhaps I had received bad news from Halle, I cried like a child, whereas up to then I had steadily controlled myself. Then Mama came, fearing terribly that one of you had died. So I had to tell her about baptism, whereupon she was extremely loving and tender and said I took everything too seriously and I would yet ruin myself with these excitements. I looked so pale, she said. She wanted to write to you and tell you to reassure me, or otherwise I would become ill. (Nonsense, of course.) Then she took me in tow on a trip into town, gave me chocolate, encouraged me, and was terribly nice. I had little strength, however. One year without you! That weighed on me like a nightmare. I was as if distracted.

But Emmy, Jesus conquers nevertheless! To Him be praise for everything! Now I am very serious, but comforted through Him. His peace is in me and carries me.—When I had written this, the lamp went out, and Mama did not allow me to ride off. I hope you are not waiting too much for this letter. This morning I received yours, with Papa's [Emmy's father's] letter, which is after all *very loving*.

It was a terrific joy to me the way the Lord has given you firmness to take up an attitude to Papa's letter. Yes, *the Lord* leads us, not people. *He* will also decide about our seeing each other again, and He will do it marvelously. He will now take us at our word and see whether we can joyfully bear *everything* for Him. We want to thank Him for His strength.

About the theology exam Papa is right. It is simply an obligation I have. In the matter of our seeing each other and writing we shall make *no promises*. But my Emmy, let us not fall into errors we have been fighting against otherwise. We want to obey our parents as long as we *possibly can*. I therefore ask you very warmly, my bride, to find strength in the Lord that we write to each other only twice a week *ordinarily*. We had after all planned to do that ourselves a long time ago. Hadn't we? Until Sunday we will still write daily to each other. Afterwards you shall decide about it. If you consider it necessary and willed by God after all, the Lord will also help us in it. I am now completely calm and full of peace. Prayer and God's Word have given me much strength today. I see it more than ever before as my duty to work mightily toward the exam now. I must do everything so that the present state of affairs will come to an end and I can take you completely to myself very, very soon. If I do my duty inflexibly and faithfully, God will do all the rest, and do it marvelously.

As to Papa's letter to me, which I send you only reluctantly, you must realize that men always write to each other as objectively as possible and leave their feelings out of it. The close is very kind and loving.

If I could only speak to my father! He is perpetually unavailable. But of course I must not precipitate anything. The way Jesus leads is the best way.

Now, my Emmy, let us gather strength over and over again in prayer and in the Word, strength to look toward Him and to trust Him in utter simplicity!

May He lead you and me in such a way that we do nothing wrong and remain always in His peace, without haste. And His Word will remain our only authority. We hold fast to nothing but *Jesus* as He is revealed to us. May He be praised from our whole hearts! He makes us happy and victorious.

Loving you in Him,

Eberhard

Breslau, Sept. 18, 1907

My beloved and highly honored Father [von Hollander],

For your serious, objective letter I thank you very much, above all for the love that I know lies behind it!

I did not think of taking a position without an exam. With your express agreement I would at the most have worked immediately toward the degree of Doctor of Philosophy. I feel quite clearly that it is my duty toward you to take my first exam in theology. On Good Friday I made no commitment in regard to my later professional activity; I did name quite a list of possibilities as independent positions. It is understood that in this too your wish and your consent is of greatest significance. In the completion of my studies, however, I simply have to keep my word. If my information is correct, that in order to take the exam I have to be a member of the established Church, I shall in no case withdraw until that time. Should believers' baptism also be an obstacle, I must and would postpone it too until after the exam.

Entirely justified as your first demand immediately seems to me, the second seems to me just as terribly difficult and hard. Yet I must not oppose it, and shall also ask my Emmy warmly to correspond only twice a week with me from Sunday on for your sake. I cannot of course give a binding promise for this second condition, however much I shall bear it in mind. As far as my sudden change of opinion on the baptism and Church questions is concerned, I myself would hardly have thought it possible in those so untroubled August days. I did however feel it my obligation to inform you *immediately* of my convictions. You cannot know *how* I have suffered because of the pain I have caused you both. I only hope you do not think that I disappointed your trust. I never wanted to appear any different than I am and think. I ask you *very* much, beloved Father, that you allow me, not merely in the interest of Emmy and your immediate family as you have written, but in any event to have a talk with you and try to gain your loving sympathy. My new position brings me one burden after another, and the heaviest of these is your distress. Nothing is further from my wish than to hold to it *stubbornly*, and I wish to continue testing most conscientiously all objections and doubts.

To close, I thank you with all my heart for the important assurance that our personal relationship will remain completely as it was, and I underline this with joyful thanks. For your warm greetings too I express my thanks and ask you to greet dear Mama, for whose health I am greatly concerned, and Emmy's brother and sisters very much.

I have a great deal of hope for our talk, for granting which I thank you very much, and in the whole difficult matter I trust in God.

As always I remain in obedient, heartfelt devotion.

Your grateful son Eberhard

Our Hold

To my Emmy!

Human supports will never hold.
Thou, Lord, art enough for us.
Christ remains when everything else breaks down.

Many kinds of darkness are around us,
Yet the Lord is our light.
Peace rests on His child.

We bear many a hurt.
It is Jesus who gives healing.
Savior, we trust in Thee.

We follow Thee, free of haste.
Thy peacefulness remains our pleasure,
Golgotha the heart's rest.

Jesus Christ is at our side,
The burden of sorrow sinks away,
Satan's cunning is overcome.

Jesus says to us: Rejoice
When you have to suffer for my sake.
Yours is the Kingdom of Heaven.

Yes, Jesus, we follow Thee!
Thy joy makes us rich.
We remain eternally Thine.

Sept. 19, 1907

Breslau, Sept. 20, 1907

1 Cor. 15:57. But thanks be to God, who has given us the victory through our Lord Jesus Christ!

My bride,

Before I tell you how happy I am in Christ, I want to thank you very much for your latest letters, for the two beautiful cards in the parcel, for the charming tablecloth and the letter for Mama [Arnold]! You strengthen me just tremendously, and I only wish that I shall be able to do that equally as well as you.

I rejoice mightily that you are more definite than I in your understanding of Papa's [Emmy's father's] demands. I do believe, however, that I did not yield too much. I hope and beseech the LORD that we two may be able to see each other again very, very soon. We do have so endlessly much to talk about, and doing this by writing is always only a halfway thing.

I can only understand Papa's request that we should not see each other for one year as a shot fired in the air to frighten us from baptism and as punishment for the pain we cause them by it. From the standpoint of reasonableness and ordinary human fairness I consider the demand totally unjustified and *wrong*. I am glad, however, that I did not see this more clearly until after I had sent off my answer, for as a Christian and a very kindly received son-in-law I owe it to Papa to put up with a great deal. Thus I believe my answer was written in the sense and strength of the Lord. By word of mouth I shall be able to reconcile more outspoken words with the devotion and love that is due. At the next opportunity I shall make it very definitely clear to your Papa that I have told him clearly *from Good Friday on* that Jesus is the sole content of my life. He could not help knowing that I am guided only by Him. Thus the state of affairs since our engagement has not been altered; it is just the same, only more pronounced, and this only on the one point.

But I am *not in the least* angry with Papa. Through Jesus I have *fully* overcome the blow of this letter and am quite calm and happy. I can really feel for Papa in his agitation and love him terrifically just because of his love for you, which among other things has urged him *very much* to write this letter. With Mama and Olga it is a little bit more difficult for me. But there too I also forgive everything with my whole heart and ascribe it to the considerable blow and to Mama's lack of self-control because of her ill health. You see, I am convinced that Papa would never have written to me as he did unless these things had been suggested to him from that side. I don't believe that this way of going about the matter comes from him. But enough about that. I love them all extremely much and pray for them all the more fervently. You of course know me better than any human being, and you know how hard every cut in this letter was bound to hit me. But you know just as well that Jesus is in me and that His love overcomes *everything*. I would like to write it to you in every possible way that I am in full peace and full love. I ask you very much to overcome this letter through Jesus even quicker and better than I. I know that it is really terrible for you, and it was horrible for me to have to send it to you. But you know what Jesus can do, don't you, Emmy? Please send it back to me soon. I need to have it again. If Papa comes to you, greet him very, very warmly from me. I shall of course travel by way of Halle in October.

Here with us everything is led so gloriously by Him that I cannot marvel enough. Mama is more loving to me than ever, and Betty and Hannah too, especially the latter. Her prayers show how she understands us and is one with us in Jesus.

Mama felt your so clear statement about our baptism as very bad news—"Job's news," as she called it—but she was very, very loving about it. Of course she hopes we will come away from it, or not have ourselves baptized until five to ten years after our wedding!! To me, however, believers' baptism is so completely clear as the only Scripture-based demand that I consider a change of mind quite out of the question. I shall also write this to Halle again soon. But I am also very much in favor of going to meet our dear parents just as far as at all possible. The baptism question is not so obvious and clear to everybody today as it was in Paul's time (Acts 22:16); even men of God who are very decided and who are Bible scholars have astonishingly divided opinions about this. I therefore feel that we must not regard Papa's demand that we wait one year with our baptism as so unreasonable *in itself.* You remember, in Else's case at that time we did say she should give in to that extent so as to prove her firmness and independence and her obedient cooperation. I would, therefore, definitely have advised you too to contemplate a waiting period of a year without making a promise—as long as God does not show you plainly otherwise—if you yourself were not so decidedly convinced of the contrary and if the impression had not unfortunately been aroused that they are trying, not to test our conviction, but to break our will by separating us. For this reason I only want to ask you that both of us still pray a great deal about it. One thing I feel for sure: as long as there is truly any question of our having opportunity to test the opposite viewpoint still more, we should yield. Further than this, however, not one step, except if there is an obligation, as in my case.[21] Now may Jesus, our faithful Lord, continue to protect you! He carries us and makes us happy.   Your Ebbo

[On a slip of paper attached to the letter below:]
                    10 o'clock, Main Railway Station

Did you receive my telegram to Frau Baehr? I sent it at about 4:30 or 4:45. Papa knows it now too. The Lord is guiding me very helpfully. I am very much in peace and in the trust of Jesus, and my family are all very loving. I trust Jesus for the future with joy and certainty. He does everything gloriously. Let everything be completely and solely for His honor, for His glory!   Your happy Ebbo

                              Breslau, Sept. 21, 1907
My Emmy, you rich child of God!

You can imagine somewhat the constant worry I am in about you. It is a hard trial of my faith to know that you are in need and struggle. I suffer terribly from it. I can only hold fast to Jesus—always. I actually wanted to travel through the night on receiving your letter so as to be with you early tomorrow morning. But I cannot, and I cannot find clarity as to whether that is right. You see, I fear that your situation will only get worse if we immediately act against your parents'

[21] Eberhard's promise to pass his exam first.

order without having given them an opportunity to modify it or take it back. I think it is better for you to represent it for now and I in a few weeks; this way I believe we will get further.

I think you will know *best now* whether it would be good for me to come tomorrow, better than you were able to know in Brumby, and far better than I can know in Breslau. So I am asking you to send me a telegram immediately on Sunday morning so that I will receive the telegram by 10 o'clock (at the latest); THEN I WILL COME RIGHT AWAY AND BE AT YOUR HOUSE BY 7:30 IN THE EVENING. But I ask you urgently to do this *only* if you are certain that JESUS WANTS IT BECAUSE I CAN REALLY HELP. We *really* don't want to provoke your parents still more, but rather to reassure them in every possible way. Really use your visit for this, my Emmy! I am constantly with you in prayer. It would have been more calming for me if you were not in Halle now since I am very thankful to God that in Brumby you don't live so much under the continual pressure of these excitements. But perhaps you are right. I am somewhat worried that you may not have fully kept your inner peace. I believe that otherwise it wouldn't have occurred to you to be baptized even *before* arriving home. This too can be Jesus' will, however, although I have weighty reasons against it, which we really should *listen* to. You won't be able to prevent Mama's threats in this way but only by prayer and love. I ask you in Jesus, my Emmy, become completely quiet before Him! I believe that 1 Thess. 4:11 is called for now for us. We shall conquer, not by hastily breaking off the difficult struggles, but by quietly listening to Jesus' leading and justice on all sides.

Let us seek to be very scrupulously fair to our parents, particularly in these struggles. May the Lord help us to do this. Please write to me very fully!

I hope you still received my last letter.

How I do feel urged to fight at your side and to support you! But let us remain perfectly sheltered in Jesus! May He protect you! He does it! Please write everything to me. I shall write you a longer letter tomorrow to Brumby. Greet your brother and sisters! Jesus conquers. To Him be glory!

Your faithful Ebbo

Breslau, Sept. 21, 1907

My *dear* Father [von Hollander],

If you had not denied it to me, I would be with you all today in order together with Emmy to clear up some points of your letter which assume a state of affairs different from that which actually exists. Now, however, I can send you this warm written greeting and ask you fervently to encounter Emmy's explanations with the loving understanding you have always shown her.

Then you too will also soon realize to what extent some of the assumptions made in the points of your letter are not actually so.

I am so infinitely concerned to show you my warm love and reverence that I find it very hard still to wait until the middle of October for my short visit. I am calm, and thankful that these difficult problems and the difference in our attitudes to them must in the end only contribute to the strengthening of our personal relationship. Please greet Mama very warmly from me!

In loving reverence,

Your always thankful Eberhard

Breslau, Sept. 22, 1907

Psalm 34:2!

My Emmy,

First of all, I thank you very warmly and full of joy for your telegram and card, the contents of which made me very glad because it was in accord with my impressions about God's will.

True, I am joyful, with trembling. For you will certainly have terribly hard days. But think of the one thing, my dear Emmy, that *Jesus* is very close to you, the Jesus who stilled the storm, who reached out His hand to Peter, who had love, help, and *strength* for everyone and has poured out His *Spirit* into our hearts! With this *Jesus* you can and must conquer everything, whatever it may be! Again and again we want to trust Him fully in prayer, and He will bless us fully.

Papa [Arnold] was loving and patient to me beyond all expectation. He was naturally not able to quote actual biblical reasons for infant baptism; he only tried to convey to me that his concept was possibly right, saying that conditions nowadays are completely different from those of that day and that we could not repeat the apostolic times but must apply the deepest of their chief principles to the present day and do this in such a way that we let conditions stay the way they are given to us. I cited Scripture again and again but did not say a great deal.

Only a few passages about baptism I set forth fully. Papa declared very plainly and definitely that there was no question of my being admitted to the exam as a "Rebaptizer." I could not be regarded as belonging at all to the established Church anymore. And he would represent personally in the most decisive way that this should never happen (that a baptized person be admitted to the exam).

You see that accordingly I must postpone my baptism until after my exam since I am obligated to the latter as my *first* temporal duty.

I am thankful that in this manner I am being guarded by the Lord's leading from any suspicion of being overhasty, and can continue to test everything in the most careful way. I am now very eager for your letter and your further decisions. How much you will have experienced!! I pray for you full of faith and joy! Jesus is close to you!

Starting tomorrow I shall again *work* with strong concentration and leave to one side everything else that is not directly ordered by the Lord. If you, my Emmy, are in agreement, I shall write to you always on Wednesday and Saturday, and perhaps you write so that on these days I will always *receive* a letter. If you at all have time, always write at great, great length! Now Jesus protect you! I am always close to you, just when we are separated. And Jesus will lead us together most marvelously as soon as that is best for us. And surely we will not need to wait too long. To Him be honor, to Him be praise and honor!

Very happy in Him,

Your joyful Ebbo

Main Railway Station 11:30

My Emmy,

God gave blessing this evening. I spoke with trust in Him. In the prayer meeting that followed some expressed their conversion in the prayer. With one man I spoke alone; he confessed sins to me and how he had almost been driven to suicide by them. He trusted completely in Jesus, that from today on he is His disciple. Let us give thanks *very* much. He is mighty to conquer if we simply *trust* in Him. I am very happy and think of you. Yet to Jesus alone be all glory. May He fill you with joy and strength! Tomorrow there will be a student conference here. Full of happiness,

Your Ebbo

Breslau, Sept. 22, 1907

My beloved Father [von Hollander],

First a warm greeting! Since the result of my inquiries is that my baptism would prevent me from being admitted to the exam, I must postpone carrying out my decision until after the latter. I am very glad to have such an opportunity to test the rightness of my conviction over and over.

Because of a very fine talk with Papa on a longer outing, the unexpected arrival of my oldest sister, and a lecture which I still have ahead of me, my Sunday has become so full that I am only able to make this short communication with you.

With very warm greetings to Mama and Emmy's brother and sisters in warmest love,

Your faithful Eberhard

Breslau, Sept. 25, 1907

Psalm 34:2!

My Emmy,

Your letters from Halle, very specially the last one, make me *very happy and thankful*. That the Lord has used your trip *so much* for reassurance and clarity makes me *very* joyful! Your dear, good parents! I hope to visit them in the middle of October. Until then I shall study quietly at home, and it is high time I did that.

My family is *not in the least* angry. Even Papa does not reproach me *at all*. He only feels we are reading the Bible for wrong purposes, so as always to have material to write to each other. As if we had to go looking for that!

Through the Lord I have already got so deeply into my studies in these days that I can only send you this short greeting. You will get something more from me this week. I am now studying chiefly Hebrew and Church history. Pray and give thanks with me that the Lord is helping. While I was praying *very much* for *you* and myself today, I became *filled with joy!* I would still like so much to write a lot to you about my great happiness in you if all three sisters were not in my room talking with the greatest zeal about a big row in Mama's coffee circle. They greet you very, very warmly.

One more wish: Please write to me when and where you always go to Church. Surely only in Calbe to Pastor Hachtmann? At what time does Church begin on Sunday? I would like very much to know.

Yesterday half a year ago you gave me your hand for the first time!!

Breslau, Sept. 26, 1907

I will praise the Lord at all times! His praise shall evermore be upon my lips!

My Emmy,

So that the mail won't let us down again today, I want to send off my little parcel today, Thursday; it is actually intended only for Sunday. I think the stationery will give you joy even though it isn't as pretty as that of Sister von Niebelschütz. I looked in five or more stores before I found anything satisfactory. The roses will remind you of March 29!

Your bridegroom

Breslau, Sept. 29, 1907

Rejoice in the Lord always! (Phil. 4:4)

My Emmy,

Today I have come in a very special way to recognize that "They who look upon Him shall beam with joy!"[21] After your delightful letter this morning, I remained at home alone, especially in prayer and undisturbed consideration. I spoke with the Lord for a long time and in doing so experienced an hour such as we do not often have, an hour in which Jesus filled me quite indescribably with His peace and with the certainty that we are with Him upon His way. I laid the baptism question before Him most carefully all over again, and through

---

[21] Just six months after their engagement.

His Word and His Spirit in deep quietness and joy, I am completely certain that we must be baptized and that this is a mercy from God. When I had read 2 Cor. 6 then, I also spoke with God for a long time about the Church, and I feel clearly before Him that I must leave the Church in order to have no part in its hypocrisy and lying. When all this had become certain to me in such quietness and clarity, I also asked the Lord very conscientiously whether I had perhaps yielded too far on the exam and the postponement. But I feel quite reassured that it was and is His way that is allowing us to wait. When I read 2 Cor. 6 in God's Spirit, especially when I read aloud in Greek, I applied each sentence to us two with great joy. Yes, Emmy, we want to conduct our lives like that, utterly and completely on the side of truth, in difficulty and yet always in joy (verse 10)! Such is the way of His servants, a glorious way following the Lamb wherever He goes!

You can imagine how I praised God today for having given you to me. And if you had heard all that I said to Him about you, you would have answered, "*Ach*, Ebbo, that's just what *you* think." But I know what I have in you, and I shall never be able to thank God enough for it.

But in everything and through everything we want always and forever to proclaim one thing only: *Christ*, and Him as the Crucified!

What you write, that Papa [von Hollander] is much more distant to you since his letter to me, hurts me very much. I pray that you may be able to forgive and forget it completely, that Papa will be just the same toward you as before. It would really be bad if we could not let ourselves be hurt without our love decreasing at all! I mean of course the love to the one who hurts one of us, hard as that may be. You know of course only too well that it is the greatest imaginable temptation to me if you are in any way attacked or treated in an unseemly way. But we both want to conquer this and help one another so that all our affairs take place with love (1 Cor. 16:14) which is closely connected with the victoriousness of faith in verse 13.

It certainly is not wrong to doubt whether someone is a child of God if *one's objection is based on the Bible.* But we must be very careful that *weaknesses* do not cause us to fail to recognize a brother. We want to *carry* the weak ones.

In these days I have often let the glorious memory of our wonderful engagement time pass through my thoughts as follows:

I was so happy when I heard at last from Frau Baehr that you were converted, for ever since my Bible class (on the how-manyeth of February?) I had really seen in you the goal of my highest wishes. When I had then decided to go to one of Kühn's meetings, the one on Sunday, in spite of my work with Loofs, I escaped from my uncle Heinrich *with difficulty* in the fairly definite hope of seeing you there. When I met you right away on the stairs, overjoyed inside, I said with the appropriate reserve, "I am very glad indeed to see you here again." You gave me your hand and said, I believe, "So am I." I offered to come for you afterwards and inquired about it. You said, however, that your brother would come for you. Then I came with Dr. Heim to sit in front of you to one side. I am amazed that I was able to go back and forth past you without any mishap while helping with the furniture. Later

I waited for you at the door, and we silently shook hands in farewell. I went back to my room, kept walking up and down, and asked Brun in strict confidence for advice as to how I could approach you in order to win you. I thought of Frau Baehr and a visit to your parents. I pinned the boldest hopes on your having given me your hand; yet these were soon far exceeded by the reality.

The next day, Monday March 25, I went very early in the afternoon to Frau Baehr with the thought of possibly opening my heart to her and asking her to invite you with me some-time. But it wasn't possible, since soon Kühn came. Frau Baehr named those who were going to come. When she named you among them, I decided, contrary to the plan I actually had for the afternoon, to stay. After the meeting, during which I was able to see little of you, I went up to you in the hallway, began a conversation about Heinz coming to fetch you, and offered to accompany you myself. You accepted this for Tuesday evening, as you had already said at home that you would unfortunately not be able to go since you had no one to take you home. I was just terribly happy about this success, and tried to slip away early that evening from my uncle Heinrich's, where I was invited. But that didn't work.

Then came that important Tuesday, March 26, the day when for the first time in our lives we were to have a real talk with each other. I didn't manage very much in the way of work. In the afternoon I was naturally at Frau Baehr's. I repeated my promise to take you home and asked whether I might come to your home already beforehand to take you there, but this you refused with thanks. After this Frau Baehr, with L. Franke at her side, drew me into a discussion, and you disappeared behind me, leaving me in the lurch in barely suppressed fury at this unnecessary talk just at that moment. But Jesus helped me to conquer. By looking toward His leading I overcame all wrong feelings and only looked out for you very closely downstairs to see if I could still catch up with you.

In the evening I hurried to Dessau Street, where to my delight I met you and Olga. I noticed that you were happy that I came to get you even though you said we had not agreed on it. Olga was absolutely winning in her kindness, which I immediately understood rightly for my encouragement. We spoke about the meetings, also right away about our parents in Breslau, and you said for you it was most important of all in the meetings that people should really mean seriously what they say. As soon as Olga was gone I said I had heard that you had now decided for Jesus, because I didn't want to lose any time. You replied, "Yes, fully and completely." Then we probably spoke about the marvel of such a life, about confession, Salzwedel, my conversion, family, etc., continuing this on the way home, when we again went along the Friedrichstrasse, Wilhelmstrasse, Ludwig-Wucherer- and Dessauerstrasse. We were both very happy and full of trust.

I prayed long and earnestly on my knees, and received from the Lord the *certainty* that you would become mine. I then went into a café on Geist Street and ate something and went off to the heath; there I experienced the most glorious night of my life in prayer and thoughts of you.

Wednesday afternoon I was naturally at Advocatenweg 5 [Frau Baehr's house], where I saw you sitting at the grand piano behind the door with Mimi. My suggestion that I would wait for you till the end, you rejected definitely. However, I was allowed to come for you the next time, and appeared in good time; I was conducted very kindly by Alwine [the maid] into Papa's study, where I looked at everything with great interest. You then came very soon, ready to go.

Very happily we went off together, speaking right away at the house door about your sisters. You told about Else ("We now have a converted sister"), about Mimi, about the spring songs you sang, and how the others had said they would like to be just as happy as you. I told about my night on the heath, which you called a marvelous thought. Then we came on the topic of Salzwedel, and the difficulty of the situation. When we were at Frau Doktor Schulze's, I said, "Correspondence can be a big help then." And then came the marvelous meeting and the meeting afterwards with your witness that you had decided completely for Jesus in those days, my joy about this in the vestibule while putting on our coats. On the way home I soon began and asked whether you would allow me a question —whether we could correspond. You said you thought that would be very nice, also just because of strengthening you. But it wouldn't work on account of the Matron. I declared that we simply must find a way. "General Delivery" was immediately rejected, and the way via your *parents*, Dessauerstrasse, accepted right away. I also said I couldn't imagine that today was the last time we would be together, and that God had not led us together for nothing. I noticed definitely that you agreed. I then spoke of my future, of your freedom as a nurse; you spoke about the mission, and we agreed that we wanted to belong to each other. Arriving at your house door, I asked

you if you thought I might visit your parents, and you said you
had been going to ask me that. I expressed my joy that you
felt the same way about it as I and that therefore we did not
need to say farewell yet. We gave each other our hands and
agreed that we were sure of one another. And after three times
twelve hours we became betrothed for ever.

But now, my Emmy, I must come back to the present, full of
happiness about you in Jesus. I think this long letter, which
surely beats the record, will help you to be content if I only
write to you briefly on Wednesday. You know that I am with
you the whole week long in my thoughts. Pray for me that I
may accomplish something and be led by the Lord. I shall do
the same for you. Jesus protect you hour by hour!

Parents and brother and sisters send warmest greetings.

Your ever faithful bridegroom

John 14:27!   Breslau, Oct 2, 1907

My bride,

I am now so mightily absorbed in study that I feel myself
completely transplanted among the original Christians with
their genuine God-made free enthusiasm and expectation of
Christ, among the Marionites with their exaggerated Paulinism
and Gnostic system of thought, among the Montanists in their
prophetic inspiration in the Holy Spirit and sharp separation
from the world, and then again among the beginning Catholics
with their acceptance of the heathen-philosophic organizational
spirit. In all this I keep wishing, "Oh, if I could just tell
Emmy about all this abundance of thought and reality!" I am

convinced it would interest you tremendously and gain your sympathy. But for now I must let it be enough to send you this warm greeting.

I take little part in the family and have had much blessing in quietness just in the last days; thus I have more joyful victory over world and sin than before, and I believe I will make a more and more decisive stand against all lying and sin.

You know, how your meaningful letters gladdened and moved me! I understand it very well that in contrast to earlier on you feel less desire to accomplish particular things, because you always think of the old impulse to ambition that is past and given up. It is good that you have made a clean sweep of this and are freed of it through Christ. But shouldn't the longing to glorify *Jesus*, to light up *Him* as the One who can accomplish more than all others, do *more* than human ambition? And shouldn't the love of Christ join much more perfectly and happily with loving service to men than self-love? I believe that out of the first reaction from ambition to distaste, the second *positive* one must come forth, from powerlessness to the power and glory of Jesus! You surely understand how I mean this. I am certain that faithful, joyful work in the daily round of duties must make you very happy and satisfied since you do them for Jesus, in Jesus, through Jesus! Therefore go forward joyfully! Thank the Lord and ask Him for strength *and joy* in your work and at your work! I am praying with you. He will give it. Are you also paying close attention, my Emmy, that your struggle with sin does not turn into brooding introspection again? Just as we are sharp and thorough in combating sin, so we should be free and lively in looking toward Jesus and share joyfully and livingly in all the little joys that surround us everyday. So ever joyful! Jesus conquers! In joyful happiness,

Your faithful Ebbo

Breslau, Oct. 5, 1907

My dear Else,

Your so loving letter to us both was a tremendous joy to me. About the future I have no worry whatever. Jesus will lead everything marvelously. I am not counting on our parents, or on Gerdtell, or on other brothers or sisters, or on offers, etc.; I simply rely on *God* and go His way, not looking to right or left.[22]

United firmly and faithfully in Him,

Your brother Ebbo

---

[22] After a time of waiting Eberhard, Emmy, and Else finally left the State Church in 1908 and accepted believers' baptism, indeed a radical break with the established order, for the sake of Jesus!

III   ELSE VON HOLLANDER

III ELSE VON HOLLANDER

"For where two or three are gathered . . ."

Any story of the origins of our Church community life should include a section on Else von Hollander or "Tata," the sister of Emmy Arnold. Apart from Else's letter, the extracts for this section have been taken from our previously published book *Else von Hollander*[1] and from memories in 1972 and 1973 of the Arnold children: Hardy, Heini, and Hans-Hermann, and of Annemarie Arnold, the wife of Heini.

1. *Else von Hollander's Development and Family Background*
as told by Eberhard Arnold on January 17, 1932,
six days after her death

The von Hollanders were among the upper-class families of Riga, Latvia. About 1890 Else's father resettled in Halle, Germany; it was the time when the Russians were beginning to take over everything. Else's father, Heinrich, was already a professor of law in Riga. He then began his studies over again in Germany, even with a family of six children.

Upper-class families like theirs represented from the outset

---

[1] Eberhard Arnold and others, *Else von Hollander: January 1932* (Rifton, New York: Plough Publishing House, 1973).

a vigorous culture along with a liberal frame of mind, but this was so conditioned by tradition that a radical change of attitude was hardly possible. It was a deeply instilled Lutheran view, based on an absolutely pure and moral life. To be sure, they took no inner attitude to private property, nor did they devote their lives to the Kingdom of God, but they did have a full and positive respect for the Bible and my father-in-law represented that those who were innocently impoverished should be helped, thereby incurring sharp criticism. My mother-in-law was very keen on the company of town councillors and pastors. But my father-in-law was anything but impressed by the entire city of Halle.

Else was very much protected in her early youth. As times grew worse and the family had to retrench considerably, they were willing to let their daughters learn something; but they were not to take up careers.

At first Else's interests were centered more on artistic things, and she therefore made the request to study art and attended various art institutes in Halle and Dresden. The Fellowship Movement then arose among the families of pastors and doctors in Halle through Ludwig von Gerdtell. Through the Fellowship Movement, Else's personal discipleship became clearer and more definite, and she soon became an apostolic witness in her family.

Then came the time when Emmy and I were to be married. Else at that time took an extremely active part in the evangelical movement. She concerned herself with the poorest people. When we were living in Leipzig, Else was at our house very often. In 1913 she became completely a part of our family, so that she also travelled to the Tyrol with us. She had a very childlike way and in deep experiences the ability to express her innermost heart. She never repeated the words of others but shaped and formed thoughts in the inward, characteristic way of her childlike spirit.

When we were in the Tyrol, it became clear to us that we must press forward to an inner life that permeates the entire structure of society. Else occupied herself with Jakob Hutter and his influence, with the mystery of the experience of God, and above all with the Bible itself. The book *Innenland* then came into being. This was the first time Else worked hard with me on one of my books.

Then came the letter calling me to the leadership of the Furche Publishing House, and in connection with this Else was then also employed as literary secretary. Else soon found her way into this work so well that I was able to entrust her with scholarly tasks of any kind; she also worked independently on the art layout for several things.

We attended a great number of Christian gatherings, and in general our inclination was to keep up the contact with them all. (In the meantime, Else had also refused a marriage proposal.) Else had a feeling for genuineness in religion, a love for nature, and an artistic talent. Altogether, Else took such an essential and unique part in everything that from this point on it is impossible to distinguish her share in the work from ours.

From then on, our whole development went ahead in one direction. The outbreak of World War I drove us from the mountains and to Berlin. Else was always in the forefront. We

knew for certain that we would not be able to achieve anything on the basis of our own intentions. This inner certainty
was one that Else had and also Emmy and I.

Our financial situation was difficult ever since we had broken
with our previous way of life. It was a principle of ours never
to take any of our money into the New Year with us. Under no
circumstances did we want to grow rich, to have a savings
account. We decided to make a break, and we were seeking in
the direction of the Early Church with its community of mutual
trust. There was no circle of friends to support us. Not one
person among us could be compared with Else.

2. *Some Memories of the Arnold Children Regarding "Tata"*

On Sunday, October 8, 1972, Heini Arnold told the New Meadow Run
household how his father, mother, and aunt led them as children to Jesus.

My memories go back to Berlin. There was a war on, and
almost every nation was against Germany. And that was very
serious for my parents and for Tata, who was my mother's
sister. We said, "Mama, Papa, and Tata." Then the war came
to an end and Germany was blockaded, and that meant that
no food was allowed to come in, and I know my father was
very distressed about the hungry children in Berlin.

So in our family we were five children; Monika was too
small to sit at the table. We were five children and Tata, and
there was always one place more set than for the size of the
family, and we asked Papa, "For whom do you set that place?"

And he said, "It is for Jesus, He might come;" and that we should then receive Him. And whoever came, a beggar or whoever, there was the table already set for him.

Then we moved to Sannerz, and my parents had very little time for us. Of course there was Tata, and a certain Suse Hungar (our teacher), and others. We felt that there was something of God that drew people to visit us. All kinds of people. The whole village was astonished. We were called the "*Neuwerk*," which means "New Work," and that is what our first magazine was called.

On October 14, 1972 at Woodcrest, Heini and Hans-Hermann Arnold told the Joint Shalom[2] Meeting of our three communities about the beginning years of the life in community.

HEINI: Now what impressed me especially in the last years, when so many brothers and sisters were taken from us, was the memory of how Tata, one of the first Brotherhood members, was called into Eternity in 1932. There was a vision shown to her of the Kingdom of God, which we can experience here on earth in an atmosphere surrounded by evil elements. On the other hand, the Kingdom of God will come and is already in existence. These words were real. We know from the words, "Thy will be done as it is in heaven." We know in Heaven God's will is already done.

Hans-Hermann was very impressed by Tata. He had the task every morning at seven o'clock to make the fire in a little stove in her room. He experienced something of Jesus there, and I can only tell you it was very strong.

It does not matter for Eternity if you join the Bruderhof or

[2] Group of the young unmarried people on the Bruderhof.

not, but it does matter for your eternal life if you follow Jesus and His atmosphere and reject all impurity, all murder, all lying. Your life depends on that and there is no escape for anyone.

HANS-HERMANN: Tata brought Christ very close. I remember one early morning she tried to share with me what she had experienced, and I almost could see what she had seen, feel what she had felt, hear what she had heard: that angels and martyrs are real, just real, present in the atmosphere, and that they come close to us if we open our hearts to them and fight for God's good atmosphere.

In November 1972 Hans-Hermann, Hardy, Heini and Annemarie Arnold told from memory of Else von Hollander:

HANS-HERMANN: Mama and Tata and Papa brought Jesus very close to us, especially through Easter or Pentecost or Christmas, which just moved our hearts for Christ. What was said brought Jesus very close to our lives, and I am very grateful that we had such parents and Tata.

In Sannerz Tata was one of those who carried the beginning of the Bruderhof life. She was a second mother to us, as a wonderful aunt; she was very loving, very simple, very modest, and warmth came from her always. When we were sick she would sit at our bedside all night through and tell us stories or sing to us, so we loved Tata very much. I always see Tata in front of me when we sing certain songs.

On the Rhön Bruderhof, the last years Tata lived among us (1927–1931) were the years when a real Bruderhof life shaped itself, with all the services and duties and carrying everything together. My father went on his American journey, and when he came back Tata was very sick. She had been in the Alps, but she felt she would only get more sick if she stayed away. Finally, when we experienced the last hours with Tata, we again felt the closeness of Eternity.

HARDY: Maybe it was in the fall after the American journey —I remember she still worked with Papa on the Hutterite manuscripts he had brought with him from America or sent on by mail, and she loved that work. When Tata was so very ill, she still worked on these old writings and enjoyed them very much.

One day I visited Tata—we often came to her or passed by her window. On that day she called out to all the young people to forget themselves, not to be so much concerned with themselves and their small world, but to give themselves to the Kingdom and to Jesus.

HEINI: She also was a child, I mean a real child. I must have been about sixteen then, and I think she woke me up in the night saying she could not sleep, that she had gossiped about Karl Keiderling, and that she had to confess to someone. I will never forget that humility; I was only a sixteen-year-old boy.

ANNEMARIE: On the day Tata had passed away in the morning, I arrived in Neuhof.[3] They told me about Tata, about her passing away. I had met her once in the school where I went with Emi-Ma. I thought it would probably be an atmosphere full of sadness and sorrow. But I will never forget; when I got to the Rhön Bruderhof (Papa spoke, probably the same night at the mealtime in the dining room), there was nothing of

[3] Railroad station near the Rhön Bruderhof.

this sadness to be felt but one could almost say a *joyful* atmosphere. One felt a real victory, and one felt Eternity had really come to that circle. That was for me something very overwhelming because I didn't have much belief; I did not really believe in Christianity or the Other World.

In the days to come, during many evenings, there were things Papa or others would tell of the things Tata had said to them and what she had hoped for for the community and for each one. It was something so real and yet so—as if it came from the Other World. It was so down-to-earth; it is hard to describe. One could also feel that the separation from her was very hard, the fact that she wasn't right there anymore. But it impressed me so much that it did not take very long to convince me that this life, and this reality which came from the Other World to men, was what I would want to seek and to follow.

3. *From a Letter by Else von Hollander,*
to Eberhard Arnold in America

Fidaz, Grisons, Switzerland
Spring 1931

The last shipment [of Hutterian manuscripts] sent in February which you packed so beautifully and where you bound everything so beautifully I left together as it was, only with bookmarks and numbers, because I didn't want to take it apart. It gave me so much joy. We—at the end Lene [Schulz] and I—have given numbers to your library books as well and entered them in a card index and two lovely catalog books.

We made three carbon copies of both these catalogs. I think you will be very glad about it when you come home! How I would love to show it all to you! But I am not allowed to come home before May. And Georg [Barth] has rebound those books of yours that were falling to pieces through so much use, and he has done it so beautifully you won't recognize them anymore. And then I copied out for you the letter from Jakob Hutter to the prisoners in Hohenwart. Emmy will give it to you when you are back on the Bruderhof, or when she finds out where she should send it to so that you are certain to get it.

What I am reading here now is *Innenland*, John's Gospel, the [Hutterian] *History Book*, and the other Hutterian writings. It is my most ardent longing that everything becomes so new in my innermost heart that only Christ—and He alone—rules in me, and that my life is there for Him, completely and at every moment, and can be used for Him, so that I shall really become one of those who wait for the day when all fight and struggle comes to an end. So I always think of you and your one healthy eye, with the wish that you come to the mission for which you have longed your whole life long, and which was always your biggest and deepest joy, and for which your heart longed in burning love for all men. How very thankful I would be if I could help a little with it. For the whole world waits for help out of its need and distress. How thankful we may really be for our Bruderhof and for that which God has done there. The last evening, when we thought of you in faith and of Hardy's and my departure, is unforgettable for me.

Dear good Emmy has nursed me so faithfully and is so wonderfully brave. And all, all, stand so firmly together.

Here my room also looks out toward the west.

Spirit fills, breaks through;
He scales the walls of mountains high,
Brings the farthest near.
He brings refreshing wind to all.

Closely bound to you in this Spirit, your faithful

Else,

who is eternally thankful to you and who after this peace and quiet will be so glad to work again.

4. *Four Poems by Else von Hollander*

I

In anguished grief,
    groan men divided all;
Though wholeness seeking,
    yet their hearts are ruled
By spirits, powers
    that separate, enslave.
When cometh unity,
    the Kingdom of Peace?

To poor, bound man,
    Thou camest as the One.
Master of Spirits,
    shed uniting light
Into our darkness,
    malice, pride, and hate.
Thou King o'er Death,
    bring life from out our death!

We stand and plead
    the Spirit from the Heights
That formed in us
    the holy Church might be.
Bring blazing fire—
    lives broken, now as one
In Thy great love.
    O Lord, come Thou soon!

Sannerz, 1925

II

Longest day of sun's bright light,
Shortest time of darkest night!
Flames of joy flare up, burst in,
Burning up all grief and sin.
> Rake now the fire together,
> In light come join your brother,
> Serving with one another
> Him, our Unity!

Hate and greed divide men all;
Over earth lies darkness' pall.
Then cam'st Thou, the world's true Light,
Waking men to live aright;
> Waked them to serve Thee wholly,
> Beat back injustice fully,
> Follow Thy Spirit only:
> Thy will be done!

O Thou never-ending Day,
Come, eternal Sun, to stay.
Bring us everlasting peace,
City bright of peace and bliss.
> Light from Thy radiance beaming—
> One Church united streaming
> Pure rays, forever gleaming—
> Glory to Thee!

Sannerz
Summer solstice, 1926

III

O mighty God, our Father,
We thank Thee from our hearts!
Protection hast Thou given
O'er land and sea afar

To him who was Thy envoy
In foreign lands unknown.
Thou gavest him fulfillment
In all his tasks for Thee.

In love the Spirit binds us
In Jakob Hutter's Church.
The Spirit binds forever
All those who witness true.

This mission Thou hast given
To gather all Thy band,
That they, united living,
Share all things from Thy hand.

Our lamps are kindled, ready;
For holy oil we plead
That when Thou, Lord, appearest,
We haste to follow Thee!

Written for Eberhard's return
from America, May 1931.

IV

Seven flames are burning in darkest night;[4]
A wand'rer far off from the distance hears
   a singing that rings loud and clearly.

They've killed seven witnesses of the Lord;
Oh, pain and suff'ring on this poor earth,
   when men cannot hear the truth spoken!

Eternal truth cannot silent be,
Else in death and pain and sinfulness
   mankind would evermore perish.

The song they sing calls new witnesses;
They follow the Lamb of God into death,
   their song means on earth they are victors!

The flames are burning on and on;
They kindle anew in every place
   the fires of love eternal.

> Found in Else's New Testament
> after her death on the Rhön Bruderhof,
> January 1932.

---

[4] In 1531 seven of the Brothers, followers of Jesus, were martyred for their faith in Gmünden, Swabia. The seven confessed their faith in a song that is still known today. In the evening of that day a traveler, on passing the place of execution, saw seven bright lights which appeared to be burning there and heard such beautiful, sweet music as though it were angels singing.

Large Chronicle of the Brothers known as Hutterians, pp. 48–50.

5. *Confession of Faith*

I believe in One God,
The Father Almighty,
And in His only begotten Son
Jesus Christ, our Lord,
And in the Holy Spirit,
Giver of new life,
And in the resurrection of the flesh,
And in one only, apostolic, holy
               Church everywhere,
Which is His Church.

This faith is redemption: eternal life! The Almighty, the Ruler of the whole world, our Father, who is in the Heavens, Jesus Christ, our Lord and Savior, the Holy Spirit who quickens, our Advocate, gives this new life to the one, holy Church through the forgiveness of sins, the sins which try to destroy us through their dark and deadly power. Only this faith frees us from the fear of death—which is not only a fear of physical death. The powers of death, the dark powers, are ruling this earth. Therefore the cry of anguish, the beseeching prayer, the groaning of the whole creation.

"Thy Name be hallowed, Thy Kingdom come, Thy will be done on earth as in Heaven."

> Written by Else von Hollander in her copy of *The Early Christians*, shortly before she came to the end of her life.
> (Earliest Coptic Confession of Faith: *see* Eberhard Arnold, *The Early Christians*, p. 127.)

IV   CONCLUSION:
OUR EMERGING BRUDERHOF LIFE

IV CONCLUSION:
OUR EMERGING BRUDERHOF LIFE

1. *What Has Become Important for Us in Jesus?*

In a talk with a guest at the Rhön Bruderhof in September of 1935, Eberhard told how the revival movement slowly dispersed and broke up because the believers wanted to find joy only in their own blessedness, without experiencing the commands of Jesus Christ in a living way through the Holy Spirit and putting them into practice.

In the discussion, the question was asked: what has become important for us in Jesus?

GUEST: I had a great shock when the revival movement disintegrated. How did that happen?

EBERHARD: I believe that there really was at that time a radiation that went out from Jesus and was received with real thankfulness as a means of personal salvation and healing; but then people were satisfied with this alone. The longing cooled off very quickly, and people were happy just to be on the way to salvation. Actually it only begins here, for Jesus says that we must be born again in order to be received into the Kingdom of God. And He shows what the Kingdom of God means. And at this point the concern for one's own person dies away.

Instead of saying, "This personal experience is given to me so that I may seek clarity about the whole of Christ and God's Kingdom, a clarity which places my life into that life which is lived for the Kingdom of God," people were seeking constant confirmation of such grace as they had already obtained.

If the Kingdom of God is in the future as well as in the present, then believers must be offered a way of life which really corresponds to the future Kingdom of God. This life will then also correspond to the historical life of Jesus Christ.

Jesus Christ is the same yesterday, today, and in all eternity (Heb. 13:8), and we must become one with Him and His future; we must live today in the way God's Kingdom will appear in the future. The Apostle says that the Kingdom of God *is* justice, peace, and joy in the Holy Spirit (Rom. 14:17). Therefore 1) it exists now; 2) it exists in the Holy Spirit, not in our good will and deeds; 3) it exists today in the same way in which it will exist in the future: as justice, peace, and joy.

This should not be limited to the soul and its salvation. This justice is certainly an inward one, and the same is true of peace and of joy, but it is not only that. It is also a justice that reveals itself outwardly as brotherliness, and a peace and a joy that become revealed to all men. With these things we have an indication of what the Kingdom of God consists in, just as we have an indication of it whenever we encounter Jesus Christ. It consists in really living in absolute peace: never taking up the sword anymore or having any possessions or going to court or having anything to do with tribunals, but only living in love. All this becomes clear in the Sermon on the Mount and also in the Lord's Prayer and in the words, "Enter by the narrow gate." (Matt. 7:13, NEB) This means, "Always treat others as you would like them to treat you." (Matt. 7:12, NEB) This is generally overlooked. [In 1974 it is even mocked.] You will be going this way only when you want for all men the same as you ask God to give you for your own life—in other words, absolute social justice and a peaceful attitude in keeping with God's Kingdom. We are emissaries of the coming Kingdom of God, serving only the one law, the law of the Spirit of God's Kingdom. How this looks practically speaking, the Sermon on the Mount tells us.

Whoever is honest and upright sees the way clearly before him. Of course, we cannot go this way without grace. Jesus indicates this when He speaks in the Sermon on the Mount of the tree and of the living life-power in the tree. Only in this way is the Kingdom of God like a living tree. And when He goes on to speak of the salt (Matt. 5:13), that is the essence, the entirely new nature given to us in Christ and in the Holy Spirit. For this reason Jesus says, "If your justice is no better than that of the moralists and theologians, then you cannot enter into the Kingdom of God." At the same time He says, "Set your mind on God's Kingdom and His justice before everything else." (Matt. 6:33, NEB)

This is the new life: to be submerged in this wind of the Holy Spirit. Then it will have an effect which embraces the whole world. Certainly, to this belongs the faith that we are living in a time of grace; for this tree wants to spread its influence over the whole world. And under this tree all mankind gathers, under the protection of this living tree. This is the will of Jesus. It is not enough to say that we have recognized that Jesus is the friend of our heart; we must show our love.

And Jesus tells us how we must show this love: "Anyone who loves me will heed my word." (John 14:23, NEB)

GUEST: It belongs to true discipleship that I do God's will everywhere.

EBERHARD: Therefore disciple means pupil. The Master shows him what he should do. When we talk about a Master of Spirits and a Master of Life, we mean the One who also masters life. The whole Christ wants the whole life. This is the decision. The evangelical movement failed because it did not take the step that leads to action.

2. *Eberhard Arnold's Search for the Will of God*

After Eberhard and Emmy had begun their married life on the foundation of the life and death of Jesus, it was their deepest longing to follow Him completely. They felt more and more in their hearts how this had to come to expression in daily life with their fellowmen. The experiences and consequences of the First World War brought to them impressions and recognitions of a revolutionary nature. Responding to a pastor from Württemberg, Eberhard reported the following about this in a meeting on the Rhön Bruderhof in 1933:

I should like to tell something quite personal. A group of young people often gathered around me, and I tried by means of Bible study and talks to lead people to Jesus. But then there came a time when this was no longer enough. It was a very difficult situation in which I found myself, and I was deeply unhappy. I recognized more and more that this personal dedication to men's souls did not exhaust what Jesus really asked —that which is truly God's will. From this time I recognized more and more the need of men, the need of their bodies and souls, their material and social need, their humiliation, their exploitation and their enslavement. I recognized the tremendous power of Mammon, of discord, of hate, and of the sword; I saw the hard boot of the oppressor upon the neck of the oppressed. If a person has not felt and lived these things, he might think such words exaggerated—but they are facts.

Then in the years from 1913 to 1917, I sought painfully for a deep understanding of the truth. It was clear to me that this purely personal approach does not truly express and fulfill the being of God. I felt that in applying this purely personal approach, this personal Christianity, by concerning myself with other individuals so that they like myself might come to this personal Christianity, I was not fulfilling God's will. During these four years I went through a hard struggle.

I searched not only in the old writings, in Jesus' Sermon on the Mount and other Scriptures, but I also sought to know especially the situation of the working classes, the poorest in society, the oppressed humanity of the present social order, both from observation and from books, and to share in their life. I did this in order to find a way that would correspond to the way of Jesus, of Francis of Assisi, and of the prophets. Those were tremendous struggles.

Shortly before the outbreak of the war I wrote to a friend saying that I could not go on like this. I had interested myself in individuals, preached the Gospel, and had endeavored in this way to follow Jesus. I felt that I had to find a way to be of real *service* to men; to find a dedication that was not only a contact between individual souls but a dedication that also sets up a form as a memorial in real life, by which men can recognize what the cause actually was for which Jesus died— *what it is about.*

The war continued and we saw ever greater horrors; we saw the condition of the men who came home. One young officer came back with both his legs shot off. He came back to his fiancée, hoping to receive the loving care he needed so badly from her, and she informed him that she had become engaged to a man who had a healthy body.

Then the time of hunger came to Berlin. People ate turnips morning, noon, and evening. And when the people turned to the officials for money or food in their need and hunger, they were told, "If you are hungry, eat turnips!" On the other hand, even in the middle of Berlin it was still possible for well-to-do "Christian" families to keep a cow and have milk when no one else had milk.

In 1917 I saw a horse fall in the street; the driver was knocked aside by the starving people who rushed in to cut pieces of the meat from the still warm and steaming body so that they would have something to bring home to their wives and children.

It was during this time that I visited a poor woman in a basement dwelling. The water was running down the walls of this cellar where she lived. Although she had tuberculosis, her relatives were living in the same room with her. One could hardly open the window, for the dirt from the shoes of the passers-by fell into the room. I offered to find another dwelling for her, but you should have heard what she said: "I'm not going to make a fool of myself; I'll die here where I have lived!" And she was already a living corpse.

After we had experienced all this, and had had the opportunity of putting our official residence with parquet floors and huge reception rooms at the disposal of working-class families, I realized that the whole situation was unbearable. I was told by the leader of the Student Christian Movement of that time, with whom I was working, that a high State official demanded of me that I should be silent about the questions of justice, about the war, and about the need that cried out to Heaven— then he and I could probably come to an understanding.

In our little meetings at our "open house" in Berlin, it gradually became clearer that Jesus' way was a practical one; that He has shown us a real way of life which is more than a way of concern for the soul. It is a way that says very simply, "If you have two coats, give one to him who has none; give food to the hungry (Luke 3:11), and do not turn away from your neighbor when he needs to borrow from you. And when you are asked for an hour's work, give two (Matt. 5:41–42). But you must strive for His justice. If you want to found a family, then see that all others who want to found a family are able to do so. If you wish for education, work, and satisfying activity, make these possible for other people also. If you say that it is your moral duty to care for your own health, then accept this duty for the health of others also. Treat men in the same way that you would be treated by them. In this is the Law and the Prophets (Matt. 7:12). Enter through *this* narrow gate (Matt. 7:13), for this is the way that leads to the Kingdom of God."

When this became clear to us, we saw that we can go this way only when we become as poor as beggars and take upon ourselves, as Jesus did, the whole religious and moral need of men. Then we become bearers of suffering, and we suffer because we see how injustice is conquering the world. We can be of undivided heart only when we hunger for justice more than for water and bread. Then we will be persecuted for the sake of this justice. Only then will our righteousness be better than that of the Pharisees and theologians (Matt. 5:20), for then, out of the tree-like strength, out of the life-giving energy of God's power of growth, we are filled with a new Spirit, a new fire, a new warmth, because we have received the Holy Spirit.

In this connection it became clear to me that the first Christian community in Jerusalem was more than a historical event; rather, *it was here that the Sermon on the Mount came to life.*

It is necessary today as never before that we renounce the last vestige of our privileges and rights and let ourselves be won for this way of total love, the love that will pour itself out over the land from the breath of the Holy Spirit, the love that was born out of the first Church community.

And so we came to feel that we could no longer endure the life we were living. Although I admit that I have sacrificed my personal health, I must bear witness to the fact that Jesus concerned Himself not only with souls, but also with bodies. He made the blind see, the lame walk, and the deaf hear. He served men's bodies and souls. And He prophesied and foretold a Kingdom, a rule of God, which was to change the conditions and the order of this world completely and make them new.

To acknowledge this, to live according to it—this, I believe, is God's command for this hour.

3. *The Expectation of a New Beginning*

Before, during, and after the First World War there was deep dis-satisfaction in large circles of the German youth about conditions in society, the Church, and the nations. This led to the formation of groups and circles of young people who earnestly, though often in very different ways, searched for a new way of life. That was the time of the German Youth Movement. There were conferences and gatherings where people tried to clarify their views and ideas. According to the report of an English friend, on July 5 of 1933 at the Rhön Bruderhof, Eberhard told about this time as follows:

After the war—after all that terrible misery—the question, "How is it to be now?" came up in widely different circles. People sensed something that could not be expressed in words. We had something in common that bound us together. We tried to understand what was happening. There was something growing. Something had to come. This longing led us together for conferences. We did not know beforehand what we would talk about. We expected something to happen. We did not come together to become clear by means of our intellect. We expected nothing from men, nothing from a leader or speaker or preacher, but we really expected something to happen from God. We had no very complete idea of what this event would be. We knew only that it would have to be in direct contrast to the present order of the world: the isolated and scattered character of today's existence, the hatred and hostility among the nations, and sin as separation. This is how it had to be. And it had to lead toward a new world of justice, unity, and love. That was clear to everyone. So it came about that some of us who knew that what was being expected had come among us in Jesus Christ, shared in this expectancy with the infinite joy, the absolute certainty, that Jesus alone is the fulfillment. It is therefore right to speak of a Christian Youth Movement.

The Youth Movement meant a totally new beginning. It meant the possibility of a completely fresh start in every respect, including all the activities of the human mind, the work done by men, and mutual help in this work; and altogether a new beginning with respect to everything related to man and creation and to the things of God and the Spirit. A radical new beginning was expected also in quite material and economic matters—a new beginning that had to be totally different from anything then in existence. This is what was called the Youth Movement.

During these early years of the twentieth century there existed a religious expectancy, an expectation of something coming to us in the future, something breaking in and taking place among us—a waiting for that which we can never make, which no generation has yet been able to make, and which also this new generation cannot make—something that can come to us only from the Other World and can be given only by and from God. That was the true Youth Movement. In this way—through the intervention of God—people came to faith in God.

4. *How the Church Community Came into Being*

Here follows a further report given at the Rhön Bruderhof in 1933 about the spiritual currents into which Eberhard and Emmy saw themselves placed in 1920:

Sannerz and the Bruderhof Community came into being

through the impact of two different movements converging on each other. One of these was the Christian revival movement which, based on the Bible, represented the Gospel of Christ for the conversion and rebirth of the individual with a view to his eternal salvation. The other movement was a movement aiming at justice. It has frequently been labeled an idealistic movement, but I do not agree with this. I have been at their conferences, and it is not true that the Youth Movement (also called the Free German Movement, *Wandervogel,* or Religious Socialist Movement) formed human ideas and ideals out of their own understanding and developed a philosophy of life with lofty ideas, which they then tried to live out. It was not like this. They were groups with a tremendous experience of nature, so that they sensed the religious mystery of God the Creator behind nature, and it was this bond of religious feeling that concerned them most. They lost themselves in nature, yet not so as to remain centered on nature—rather they sensed something religious that connected everything, and in it felt God the Creator.

The second experience of this Youth Movement was the community experience of the hiking or "wandering" group. This was not an experience of individuals hiking in twos or threes in the woods or on the heath, but something given to small groups, who went out into nature and sensed a mysterious bond with God the Creator behind nature and behind the communal experience of their group, which could only be explained as something of God. Community exists wherever true life pulses—community with the mystery of creation and community among the creatures, among the spirits of men.

This movement, then, confessed: We do not seek God apart

from nature, nor do we seek Him within nature itself. Rather we must go out into nature in order to experience the mystery behind it. These people reached out for the Spirit, and as they had already sensed God as the Creator, so now they sensed the divine Spirit. They felt that no true community was practicable and durable unless the Spirit united the group. There was a longing in these circles comparable to the longing of the first Christians before the Holy Spirit was poured out. There was a suspense, a cry of longing from those who waited for the Spirit to reveal Himself as the power which frees and which awakens community.

This was the point where the revival movement, concerned with the salvation of the individual, was bound to collide with the movement of young people who were seeking the deep meaning of life in and behind God's creation. It became clear that both of these movements lacked a final and complete fulfillment, and both had a burning longing for the truth of the Spirit.

So it came to this holy and quite indescribable encounter in which both these movements experienced an imparting of the Spirit, a Pentecost. The mystery of how the original Church came into being was this: after Jesus had left His disciples, He became revealed as the Risen One, as the King of His Kingdom, as the One who restores creation, who conquers and rules in order to establish justice, peace, and joy. Then through the Holy Spirit, Jesus imparted to His Church the work He had lived for and perfected: in Jesus, community was revealed. So both the longing for the mysterious harmony and unity in creation and the desire for the Holy Spirit found fulfillment in Jesus Christ. What is more, it was a fulfillment in the apostolic sense that this longing cannot grow feeble and weary, and the eyes must remain open for sober reality, and the will to justice must rise in opposition to all injustice. This fight of the early Church was against injustice, against lying and impurity, against money and possessions, against ownership, against everything that is opposed to God. All this was possible only through complete unity in God the Creator, in the incarnation of His Son, and in the outpouring of His Holy Spirit.

It is shattering to know that there are so many Christian movements which emphasize one or the other aspect of Christianity; and that this penetrating of the whole truth, completely, comprehensively, and entirely, is very seldom met with. And just that is what God has demanded of us. We cannot say of ourselves that we have achieved it. We are not equal to it. This is what is demanded of the whole of creation, the whole of nature, the German nation, of all nations: that truly God, the will of God for creation, the will of God for nature is revealed. That will truly happen, however, only when the Holy Spirit descends on us and reveals to us the final Kingdom of the ultimate future. In this Kingdom, God is victorious over all worlds and takes possession of them in complete justice and perfect peace. God, and no one but God, will do that. And therefore the Church is placed into this world as an embassy established by the Holy Spirit so that it may proclaim and put into practice this new Kingdom of transformed nature, reborn mankind—this Kingdom of joy and love and peace and justice. The only way this is possible is through the forgiveness of sins —Christ is revealed through this as the perfect Redeemer, who alone is the center, not only as the King of the coming Kingdom, but as the heart and head of His Church.

This became clearer and clearer to us at that time. We became part of the Youth Movement, and wherever we sensed any urge toward living together in community, we were glad. There we felt a spark of God, or at least a spark of the first creation as the Creator meant it to be. So we went out among men, and we got to know all aspects of human nature. And wherever men showed a sincere longing and struggling for justice, we tried to sharpen and purify it so that in fighting for the good they might hate evil without hating and wanting to destroy the evil person. And so over several years we were able to experience that we were not only visited but also urged on and supported by various circles of the Youth Movement.

We will never forget what a completely new venture this was. It has much to say to us at this hour if we have ears to hear. The challenge to recognize the Kingdom of God, the rulership of God in all things was of decisive influence for our beginning, for the growth of our small Church community, for Sannerz. The healing of individual souls belongs to it, belongs right in it; only it is not the individual man who is the center of what happens, but rather God's heart, which asserts itself and prevails in His rulership, in His Kingdom over all worlds.

God wants to enter into His rulership; in Christ, His Kingdom shall gain a footing and overcome everything else so that nothing else has or retains any importance anymore. This message should not be understood in a sentimental way. It should not be understood like this, that only the Kingdom of Heaven in the *individual heart* is important and all other kingdoms lose their importance, or that we are allowed to do everything else as long as we strive first and foremost for the

Kingdom of God and its justice as an abstract principle. (Matt. 6:33) It is not meant like this. For the message of the Kingdom of God says this to us: the Kingdom of God comes even quite independently of you, the Kingdom of God comes without you altogether; God will enter upon His rulership in Christ quite apart from your person and will conquer and take possession of everything through His Spirit. You matter only insofar as you are called to be part of it and to put yourself at His service.

5. *Some Historical Parallels:*
Anabaptism, Hutterianism, Zinzendorf, and Others

In his search for a total discipleship of Jesus, Eberhard concerned himself with the Christian movements of past centuries. In a Household Meeting at the Alm Bruderhof on August 29, 1934, he said the following about Graf Zinzendorf and the Moravian Brothers of the eighteenth century in relating them to the earlier Anabaptists of the sixteenth century:

The song "Christian hearts in love united" by Zinzendorf, which we often sing in our inner meetings, comes from the Moravian Brothers of the eighteenth century. This song originated at a lovemeal similar to ours today. Count Zinzendorf also had made an attempt at communal living, although it was not so full as that of the Brothers who are called Hutterians. In Canada there was once a Moravian mission Church which developed into a very firmly united community of work and love, almost as full as that of the Hutterians. This Canadian community had sought contact and exchange with the Hutterians. In the experiences of the Moravians and the Hutterian Brothers, we can see quite clearly what was meant by the early Christians of the first apostolic time.

The powerful movements in England at the time of Oliver Cromwell—the movements of the Independents, the Quakers, and the Baptists—were in innermost contact with the old Anabaptist movement which had arisen in Holland and in Germany; they were in contact with that Anabaptist movement which had emerged in the sixteenth century, that is, a hundred years earlier.

The original Anabaptist movement in Zürich and in Chur, and later in Tyrol and Moravia, was powerfully gripped and moved by Jesus Christ to seek justice just as much as the inner, religious life. The first demand made by the Brothers in Zürich and Basel was the abolition of interest, that is, of interest-bearing capital or modern capitalism. The second demand made by the Brothers was that each brother had to share with the other brothers all that he had, and that this be done out of love. This began in the year 1525. Already in 1528 original Hutterianism began to extend this idea, this demand with its consequence of total community of goods. First they said, "Share with your brothers!" And it was not yet quite recognized that people must also live and work together. Then in 1533 Jakob Hutter took over the leadership of this small group and built it up so clearly in full community and led it so courageously towards martyrdom, that this undertaking became invincible. The whole time of the Reformation was a powerful time of awakening.

Everywhere men were awakening to divine truth and to divine love. Historians like Ludwig Keller and Johann Loserth say in their writings that this movement is the real brotherly movement, which demands a practical life of discipleship just as urgently as it demands the innermost experience of Christ's salvation in the heart. Therefore to this day historians call it the Brotherhood Movement. Brotherliness or brotherhood means that the whole of life is placed in the light of true brotherliness. Then the sense of brotherhood penetrates everything one does and experiences. And so it must be understood that out of this powerful movement of the Reformation grew the Hutterian Brotherhood with many thousands of members, perhaps around fifty thousand. Exactly how many is not known.

Zinzendorf himself had gone through the school of German pietism. The individual soul should become certain of its Savior and joyful in Him. And each individual soul had to go through repentance and conversion before finding this faith and this redemption. Repent and believe in the Gospel! And further: each individual soul had to renounce worldly things. But pietism did not go so far as to demand that each Christian should also entirely renounce Mammon and bloodshed, fight against religious egotism, and lead toward a common dedication to the Kingdom of God. Pietism did not go as far as that. Count Zinzendorf said, "We must overcome pietism and still keep all the God-given powers it contains." And so Count Zinzendorf founded experiments in the common life. He said, "If the whole life is in common, then it will be genuine and free from all artificial piety; then the individual will no longer revolve around his own self. All will dedicate themselves together to God's cause. Piety and religious introspection will then be overcome."

In this way it came about that with Count Zinzendorf and his communities, the question of justice and the question of the economic system were just as living as the religious question

itself. It was given to Count Zinzendorf to lead the way beyond
pietism through the bold enterprise of a communal life. And
it was given to the Hutterian Brothers to lead the way beyond
the entire Reformation movement to full community living, as
it had been revealed in apostolic Christianity.

6. *How Eberhard Came to the Baptizer Movement*

Very early in his life Eberhard studied the Baptizer Movement of the
sixteenth century, a movement that stirred and gripped Eberhard and
Emmy Arnold very deeply and brought them to search in it for the true
discipleship of Jesus Christ.

At the Rhön Bruderhof on December 26, 1934, Eberhard said the
following:

I was directed to the Baptizer Movement of the Middle Ages
already by my father. He said, "The Baptizers of Reformation
times were undoubtedly the clearest of all!"

I asked, "What is your opinion of these men?"

"According to research into Church history, it is quite clear
that they cannot be thrown into one pot with Thomas Münzer.
Particularly in Moravia, a radical, upright life of love came
into being, which was actually very wonderful." He said that
Loserth in particular had written the best books about this
and that he was the most thorough academic historian we
had in the universities.

I said, "I don't understand; why aren't *you* with the
Baptizers?"

"It's quite a different matter whether I give you scholarly
information or whether I have it in my own house." There
we were back in the old fight, and he maintained that the

fact that these people were then finally driven out of Moravia and destroyed violently by the authorities was proof that it was not the will of God! I had already received enough inner light from Christ to be able to say, "I cannot understand that! Then the Cross of Christ would prove Jesus wrong!"

Then many years passed, during which I heard a great deal at the university, and my Uncle Heinrich in particular included so much in his lectures for a course which he called "The History of Sects." Here again it was the Baptizers of the Reformation who, besides the Quakers, made the strongest impression on me. At the same time I mingled with the most varied Christian circles of the present time, and nowhere was I completely satisfied. Everywhere we had the feeling: there is a grace of God at work here, truly a part of the Gospel; but it still isn't the whole of life. And so I went on seeking.

We realized more and more clearly and deeply that it couldn't be sufficient just to have contact with present-day members of living movements. The organism of the living Christ is to be found just as much among those witnesses to truth who have been called home and glorified. That is why I have always been concerned to recognize the living thread of the Christ-nature down through the centuries. That is why we lay the greatest stress on grasping the living essence of Christ's Spirit in every era. And so I was led again and again to the Reformation Baptizers, to the Waldensians, and others, but very particularly to the Reformation Baptizers. And then came the time when we started our new life.

What impressed us most then was the Sermon on the Mount and the Acts of the Apostles. For years previously, we had been influenced mainly by the Gospel as expressed by Paul, nor did we want to give up any of that. We wanted the proclamation of salvation through the Risen Christ to remain our central fire. We felt that now the Gospel of His words and deeds must move much more powerfully into the midst of this central fire. We felt it would be unbearable for us to go on living in the same circumstances—an ordinary middle-class Christian life. This is how it came about that we set out afresh in a life where everything was communal, a life based on the Sermon on the Mount, with no financial security whatever; and in this same way we came into contact with Blumhardt.

We felt the way everything, all of life, was cut into fragments was a sign that modern civilization is on the road to ruin, and we were deeply shaken by it. In religious circles it is said that the Gospels are meant for the Jews, the Letters of Paul are meant for Christians, and the Revelation has significance only for the future.[1]

A sharp separation is made between what is purely religious on the one hand and economic life and the question of justice on the other. Again we had a vision of a life that was one whole unity. As in a prism of God, all the different rays— the rays of religion, economy, and justice—were to be drawn into one unity through the true, divine, and all-embracing Spirit.

We received letters from an American professor and an article called "The Suffering of the Hutterian Brothers in the First World War," and I published these in our periodical in 1921. We then gradually tried to get into correspondence with the Brothers because we thought: since we have come to know

[1] This reflects some of the theological thinking of Europe at that time.

all the other attempts at community living, we should get to know the American community attempts too—the Doukhobors, and also the members of the Amana Community of True Inspiration, and also the Brothers. They themselves say they are Brothers and only add, to distinguish themselves from others, the Brothers called Hutterians. They do not want to be named after a man. They want to live as brothers; that was my strong impression. When I compared their life with what we have experienced, and when I thought about our own attempt at community, I saw how the Brothers were able to set us endless examples and give us no end of help for our life and its organization, whereas I was very deeply disappointed with the Doukhobors and the Amana Inspirationists. True, among the latter there was still much life to be felt, but it was not intensive, strong, objective, and substantial enough; it had already lost some of its fire. They stem from Zinzendorf's time, the time of the Wetterau Inspirationists. We also have [some of their] documents here in the house.

Then too, I visited the Doukhobors, and they were still less lively than the Amana Inspirationists. They were so full of heathen ideas, especially the idea that only one power exists in the universe. Their community was not really alive, strong, and powerful in an inner way, but very slack and not very convincing. The Hutterian Bruderhofs, however, convinced me most deeply that here the three articles of the Apostolic Confession of Faith had grown into a single unity: creative life, life redeemed by the full forgiveness of all sin and all error, and the good life of the Holy Spirit arising out of the powers from the future world. This was given there in a wonderful unity such as I had never encountered at all in present-day Christian groups in Europe, a unity that does not depend on the spirit of the times.

We were stimulated by the events of today for our own life together, and we also felt responsible for those people who were moved by the communal life. Our main question was that there was no unity in the life of Christians. This seemed to find its clearest and most genuine answer—for the present as well as the past—in the communities of the Hutterian Brothers. Our deep concern was then to seek inward and outward uniting and community with the Hutterian Brothers, who were giving the clearest and fullest picture of a life united in Christ.

7. *The Early Christian Witness Has Never Come to an End*

In a meeting on September 24 of 1933 at the Rhön Bruderhof, Eberhard Arnold said:

It is a wonderful fact that throughout the centuries the witness of the Living Word has resounded again and again in Christianity, and the Lutheran and also the Reformed Church have become guilty of an unbelievable twisting of the historical facts by acting as if the truth of the Living Word were extinct and the Christians had been wiped out. On the contrary, it must be stated that the original Christian witness and life has never ceased to exist and that in many movements and many countries it has again and again sought expression.

In the objective witness of the Brothers called Hutterians

it was clear that what is decisive is the living Word of God in the heart, the life-giving Spirit in the depths of faith. There is no community without this personal experience of the Christ speaking within us. It is impossible for us to come to real community with Christ and with God except by such a visitation of God in our hearts and souls. Each one must be gripped and overcome by the Spirit in his innermost being. And the justification by faith of which Luther likes to speak so much, almost to the exclusion of everything else, becomes then an experience of the heart. The justification of the sinner that makes him righteous before God and men is a deed of God taking place in man's inner being. Certainly, this deed of God is based on the historical facts of Christ's birth, His life, His suffering, His execution, and of the outpouring of the Holy Spirit on the Church. But we must receive this basis in our hearts.

The whole history of Jesus, from the very beginning to its final conclusion, must be repeated in our lives. Everything that happened to Jesus must happen with us. This begins already with birth. Unless, just like Mary, we receive the Holy Spirit in our inward being through the faith of our hearts, the Word that is eternally alive with God will never take on flesh in us and in our lives. Through the Holy Spirit and His uniting with the faith of our hearts, the eternally living Word wants to become flesh again and take on form and shape in us and in our lives.

If what we are taught about Jesus does not gain complete power over us and over all we have, it is of no use to us. It is no help to us unless we experience within ourselves the way of suffering that Jesus went, right to the Cross—to the betrayal, the restoration of Peter, the suicide of Judas, the for-sakenness of Jesus on the Cross, His execution by the majority of the excited mob. His whole suffering had this one meaning: it was perfect love—in perfect love He took the world-wide suffering of bleeding humanity upon Himself. We shall be one with Christ only when we in the same way receive within ourselves the whole world need and atone for it, when we, as representatives so to speak, suffer death for whatever horrors are committed. As Christ died, so we must die. Through the power of His death we must die every day. On the way of this world need, we must be ready every day to take the utmost humiliation upon ourselves, in the same way as Jesus took it upon Himself in utter God-forsakenness, on the Cross between the criminals. We must be ready to be hanged as He was hanged, to be put to death by fire, water, or the sword. Only then shall we be able to receive the strength of resurrection, the wonderful power of resurrection, for God cannot allow love to remain lying in the grave. That alone is justification when the whole life of Jesus is planted and un-folded in us anew. And just then we shall also experience the outpouring of the Holy Spirit, as it was experienced by the first Church of the first Christians. This simply meant that these first Christians were ready to receive the life of Jesus anew. The Word became flesh (John 1:14) and became Spirit again.

Faith in the Holy Spirit is a very strange thing. The Holy Spirit is something so precious that unspiritual people are un-able to draw near to Him. Just for this reason the Holy Spirit in His uniqueness must become fully revealed in the Church of Jesus Christ. In the Hutterian Church, this takes place through faith in the unity given by the Holy Spirit alone. The Holy Spirit lays before men the whole cause of His Kingdom: the Gospel of Jesus Christ, the Holy Writings in both the Old and New Testaments, the prophets and apostles of the Kingdom of God—as God had planned and decided it from the beginning of creation, and as it is revealed in the rule of righteousness over all the world. And because the Holy Spirit is so objective that He reveals to us the whole cause of God the Creator, of Christ the Redeemer, and of life eternal in the Holy Spirit, He brings total unity.

When we really and truly believe, it means that the Holy Spirit frees us from our own small personalities. Believing in Him means that He takes us right into the cause of God and unites us with all those who have represented Him; those who really represent the cause of God today and who one day, when all things shall be fulfilled, will really represent this cause. The Holy Spirit is union with the prophetic witness as well as with the apostolic witness of the Spirit of Christ in the early Church. Above all the Spirit is complete oneness with the revelation of the last Kingdom. "He will remind you of everything I have told you, and He will make me stand before you in radiant light. And He will make known the future." So the Holy Spirit proclaims the cause that was taught and lived out by Jesus, the cause which at the end of days, in God's future, will become manifest in His Kingdom. That means complete unity with the Holy Scriptures, with every word of the apostles and prophets, complete agreement with everything written in the sacred Writings and complete unanimity among all, that is, among those who are gripped and led by the Holy Spirit.

People who think of this faith in the Christ living in men's souls, this belief in the outpoured Holy Spirit, as merely personal and as leading everyone into utter loneliness, show that they do not believe in the Holy Spirit, but only its reflection in the mirror of the heart of the individual. They do not believe in the cause which is reflected in this mirror. The true Church believes in the cause, and regards the mirror of the heart as merely a receiving station, as a place, a dwelling for this cause—no more and no less. In the Hutterian Church it became manifest that this innermost revelation is at the same time a revelation that unites all believers. It is the unity (a unity that finds expression in life) of all those who really believe and have really received life. The consequence of faith is complete unity, that is to say, complete unity in the teaching and life of Jesus Christ and in the future of His Kingdom as taught by the Holy Spirit.

Let us think of the parables of Jesus. The seed of the Living Word is so small as to be invisible. But it is so full of life that it grows into a great tree (Mark 4:31), overshadowing the whole world, visible and tangible as the incarnation of the Word, the embodiment of the Unseen. And this was given to the Hutterian Church. Where true faith is revealed in the innermost heart, it has to become active in love; it has to manifest itself as complete unity of work and life; and it has to be disclosed before all the world as the mission of Jesus Christ, which manifests unity. The prayer that all may be one (so that it can be recognized by their unity what Jesus' mission is); faith in Christ and faith in the Holy Spirit; and faith in God, who in the Holy Spirit is in Christ—all this is to become manifest in a unity that is proved real in life. The cause must prove itself in life as real. For this reason community may not be restricted to the so-called invisible things—to the written Word, prayers, and the songs that are sung. For the true Church, speaking, praying, and singing belong to the Holy Spirit, who penetrates into material things. They are in place only when proved in life by the daily work, only when there is complete unity in the daily work. Only true unity, as demonstrated in community of work, life, and goods, may proclaim the Word before God. Praying, singing, and preaching are out of place where this unity is not given in practical work and in the administration of goods. That is the Hutterian conception of the Christian life.

8. *The Significance of the Blumhardts*

Eberhard and Emmy Arnold felt and believed that wherever Jesus proves that He is alive a struggle breaks out between the Spirit of God and the spirit of Satan. In their attitude of faith as regards this fight of the spirits, two prophetic men—Johann Christoph Blumhardt (father) and Christoph Blumhardt (son)—had a decisive influence on the life of Eberhard and Emmy Arnold. This spiritual direction was so decisive for Eberhard Arnold that in his last letter, which shows quite clearly that he had a foreboding he might die, he wrote the following words as a last request:

I hold firmly to the inward and outward uniting of *genuine old Hutterianism* with the *attitude of faith* of the two Blumhardts and with the life-attitude of the true *Youth Movement* as a real and wonderful providence for your future; whereas I regard a merging of Hutterianism with modern pietism as a misfortune. The Baptist Church ought to be sufficient warning to us.

In an inner meeting held on August 2, 1935 at the Rhön Bruderhof,
Eberhard spoke as follows about the significance of Johann Christoph and
Christoph Blumhardt for our community life:

We stand here in the struggle to which the father Blumhardt
was called. The father is doubtless the more original one of
the two. The son Blumhardt is more important because he
applied the father's faith to class distinctions in society and to
the question of justice, but the father is considerably more
significant because he brought to so-called Christianity something that called for decision. Let us be glad and thankful
that we have not been taken out of this struggle of the spirits,
for that would be a sign that death rules among us. The fiercer
the fight of the spirits flares up among us, the clearer it is that
Jesus Christ lives among us. But we are called so that the truly
victorious Spirit shall triumph completely; all of us together
are called to this.

And for you, R., it is also very much on my heart that you
are called to represent the Spirit of light over against the spirit
of darkness with a wakeful heart, with a loving heart, a heart
fully alive. And as with R. so it is with everybody else, whoever he may be. And there is no respite in this struggle. Awake
or asleep, at work or at rest—always and everywhere we have
to wage this holy fight. And so we want to stand together in
the faith that the Spirit of light and clarity will be victorious
over the spirit of darkness and gloom. Everywhere the Spirit
of perfect light and perfect clarity shall gain a complete victory
over the spirit of darkness and heaviness in everybody, named
or unnamed, in our circle. We must come to faith in the true
God, the true Spirit! When we believe that *HE* is, victory

has been achieved. We must be completely clear about this. Now in this historical moment it is of decisive importance that we have a completely unbroken and pure faith, a really life-giving faith in the living Christ as the life-giving Spirit. Everything dead and decaying, everything that is corrupt and leads to corruption is completely done away with, and the Spirit of life is victorious. And this takes place in the name of Him who was born of Mary and was executed under Pontius Pilate—in the name of Jesus Christ.

In March 1932, Eberhard and two other brothers went to a Religious Socialist Conference in Bad Boll in Württemberg. This was the place where Johann Christoph Blumhardt and his son Christoph Blumhardt had worked for over seventy years for God's Kingdom. Eberhard reported about his impressions of Bad Boll in a meeting at the Rhön Bruderhof on April 3, 1932, as follows:

Still today there is a lively memory of the son, and a memory of the father Blumhardt that has not yet faded completely. And we were glad to be allowed to meet with this memory as a living force for the present day.

The father, Johann Christoph Blumhardt, came from the Mission School in Basel and from the old believing circles into a parish dominated by much unbelief and superstition. He had a great love for the people and was extremely faithful in visiting them in their houses; in this way he concerned himself with all of them. Yet because of his background he kept a broad view of the whole world.

When it came to a tremendous conflict with unbelief and all such things, his view broadened afresh. He saw clearly: if Jesus wins a victory here, this victory will not only have significance for Möttlingen and the little congregation here, a victory in which Jesus conquers a possessed woman; but in this victory the Devil will be thrown back all along the line, into the utmost parts of the world; this victory will have the greatest significance for the whole of world history. The struggle was a struggle for the Kingdom of God, a struggle for the Light to conquer the darkness, for Jesus to become Victor. This little victory was to have its effect on the whole world. Here something had to happen which would bring a basic defeat to the whole demonic world so that the Devil's works would not come up again, and this not only in Möttlingen but throughout the world.

Now in believing circles in Württemberg there had developed a strong and deep direction that stood very much in contrast to the superficial fellowship movement. Through Bengel[2] and Öttinger,[3] as well as through Beck,[4] a deep interpretation of divine faith in the powers of the future was given, so that in those circles with which Johann Christoph Blumhardt had contact we cannot speak of the danger of thinking only of personal blessedness. When Öttinger said, "The ultimate of all things is physical reality," when again and again Beck's words speak so decisively of the greatness of God's Kingdom, it becomes clear that in those days the old pietists were not nearly so one-sided as to think only of their own souls being saved, as pietism of today represents. With Blumhardt it happened that people were healed, devils were

[2] Johann Albrecht Bengel (1687–1752), Swabian pastor and biblicist.
[3] Friedrich Christoph Öttinger (1702–1782), influential Swabian mystic and pietist.
[4] Johann Tobias Beck (1804–1878), Swabian theologian and biblical realist; like Bengel, expected God's Kingdom to come on earth.

driven out, and the emotionally disturbed were cured. It finally went so far that Möttlingen had to be left behind [mainly because of restrictions demanded by the State and the State Churches].

Then Blumhardt went to Bad Boll. Besides his wife and children, he also took with him Gottliebin [Dittus] and her brother and also Brodersen, who later married Gottliebin. Little by little a small living community of fifty people including children, was formed.

Friends told us that already the father, but also the son, guarded very carefully the laying-on of hands; it was free from any kind of magic power or sorcery. Both the father and the son were so clear in this area that no one could possibly make this mistake. Neither the father nor the son Blumhardt would allow the slightest possibility that any kind of magic power was present in the laying-on of hands. Just as baptism in itself achieves nothing at all unless the new birth has already taken place, as we saw today, so it is also with the healing of sicknesses. No magic effect of any kind should be expected. Not even the tiniest bit of psycho-physical influence can be tolerated in this area. Rather, it is an expression of faith.

And of what faith? This faith: that when healing takes place (however hard it is), when devils are driven out (however devilish it is), the direct personal relationship of one person to another is not what counts. The Church must be part of it. The laying-on of hands is a sign that God uses the Church for a decisive act of faith, in which God does something tremendous.

Therefore already in his day the father, Johann Christoph, came to the forgiveness of sins through the authority of the

Church with the laying-on of hands, the forgiveness which he pronounced in the name of Jesus Christ. It is significant that the healing of the sick diminished more and more during the last years of his life because there was reason to fear that the aspect of prayer-healing would come more and more into the foreground. The son continued the healings for a time, but not for very long.

There were several sons of Johann Christoph Blumhardt. Two were especially outstanding, Theophil and Christoph. Theophil was the one who was expected to become his father's successor. At first no one thought of Christoph. When he returned home from the University of Tübingen and asked what he should do, his father said, "Well, you've been living in such a grand style, I can't use you. You can wash bottles." And he put him in the wine cellar. "You can't live with us; you can be a guest."

So for about half a year he was a guest and washed bottles and so on; his father then felt that Christoph might yet amount to something. He gradually drew him into things. Toward the end of the father's life everybody was wondering very much who would actually be given the service. Then the father said, "It is Christoph." Theophil became a pastor in a village near Bad Boll, and the actual service was given to Christoph.

At first he worked completely in the manner of his father. He came to breakfast in his dressing gown and then spoke with the people in the old, pietistic way.

Gradually a new vision of God's Kingdom grew in him. I asked all kinds of people what was the essential difference between the father and the son Blumhardt. What finally came out of it was that basically there was no essential difference.

True, the father disclosed the power of evil and stood in the midst of a sharp personal fight against evil; whereas the son, while maintaining this fighting position, nevertheless wanted to see how God accomplishes His victories *in the world*—his deep concern was the problem of justice. There is a distinction here, but let us not forget that the father regarded this fight with evil as a historic event over the whole earth. He believed that real victories of the Spirit were being won even before the Last Judgment.

Blumhardt the son freed himself more and more from pious language, from the organized Church, and from pietism. He said he had had to give up these three things. The result of this freeing was that he now had an ear to discern in the history of the world where God wanted to show the Kingdom of Justice, the victory over evil spirits. He had the impression that, just as at the time of the Pharisees, "nothing can be expected of the pious people." He expected it from the "farmer lads," not from the pious. And so he looked around more and more to see whether the victory of Jesus might make itself felt among the nonpious. He was not a fighter for justice in the ordinary sense, but he did believe that God's justice would be revealed. He believed that the help for the working class must be given in that God's Kingdom is made manifest. In *this* way he wanted to see a victory won over the demonic powers; this was what concerned him. The result was that the pious people, like the Pharisees in Jesus' time, turned away from him.

He warned everybody again and again neither to imitate nor to overestimate Bad Boll as a place and not to overestimate Christoph Blumhardt. His warning was of little use.

We heard several testimonies from people who had lived

with Blumhardt. One concerns the communal work. There were sulfur pits, and two workers had unfortunately left the blow lamp down there. When they went down again to fetch it, gases had developed, and the mechanic called up for some brandy to be given to the men. And then Blumhardt fetched the gardener, and the gardener climbed down and brought one of the men up. When he went down a second time to fetch the other man, he himself succumbed to the poisoning, while the other man died of the effects of hydrogen sulfide.

Then Blumhardt, for the rest of his life, cared for Mrs. Ehrath, the wife of the gardener. It took her four and a half years to recover from this blow. Blumhardt bought her a boarding house in Freudenstadt, which was to support her for the rest of her life. This woman received very vivid impressions from the life and witness in Bad Boll, and she told me a great deal. She was particularly glad about my witness; she said it was a witness like that in the time of Blumhardt. This was a story by a member of the household.

There was also the son of a university professor, who had suffered from serious temptations in his youth. He had got to know the demonic powers in such a frightful way already in his youth that he had been in serious danger of taking his own life. From his parental home he had been endowed with the best faith, but he was by nature a very fearful person, who always expected the worst. His temptations alternated with periods of exuberance during which he felt like a demi-god. The intervals between the periods of temptation and unhealthy exuberance he spent in sadness, and in these periods he produced his scientific works. However, these intervals were quite short.

This man came to Bad Boll after having lived in this unbearable condition for many years. In Bad Boll he encountered Jesus, and the Spirit of Power freed him from the powers of the demons. He was redeemed and liberated, a man burning with fire. I saw this man myself, and he read his story to me from ten closely written pages. To be quite exact, he confided in me as in a father confessor. He felt such a strong affinity that he sought me out again and again to talk things over with me. This was an absolutely unforgettable hour for me. Of course this old Doctor of Philosophy is not healed in the sense that the sickness is no longer noticeable at all. But he is able to work and no longer needs sedatives. Before, he was able to sleep only with the help of strong sedatives. Once, for example, he had such a bad case of boils that he had to go through an operation that endangered his life. Even though he was in deep anesthesia and was unable to move, yet he felt everything. And in these moments he prayed that God might release him from this body. These are miraculous things, and there are many to be seen.

The closer circle of Blumhardt friends, which consists of only a few hundred people, does not belong to the Religious Socialist League or to the Religious Socialists, and they feel certain misgivings about this group, for two reasons. The Religious Socialists took out of Christoph Blumhardt's witness its application to the message of justice and made this into the main thing. Whereas Christoph Blumhardt expected everything from the Holy Spirit (also for the problem of justice), the Social Democrats, on the other hand, run the danger of expecting everything from their politics. Blumhardt did not think this way at all; he expected, for the problem of justice as well as for everything else, an act of God in history, a powerful intervention from God.

In regard to the true Church and unity, Christoph Blumhardt had freed himself more and more from the organized Church. However, he did not experience the real unity of the true Church in his circle, except in rare instances. Much was still lacking here. The fact that the essential nature of God's Kingdom must be manifested through the true Church was glimpsed, but this was not achieved. The Blumhardts knew, however, that their authority came from God's Church; they approached everything that happened and experienced everything in the name of Jesus Christ.

The great thing, as especially Leonhard Ragaz showed, is that here in Christoph Blumhardt was a man who did not live as if he had complete power in himself; it was a fire from Jesus, a likeness of Jesus, that radiated from him. Here was a man who saw and expected something from God for all life's problems and for every historical event; a man who had a great vision for the whole of God's Kingdom and who yet took pains and stood up for every individual.

Blumhardt the father and Blumhardt the son were both men who lived completely for the Kingdom of God; for them the reality and the greatness of God's Kingdom were more important than anything else. At the same time, they had a deep personal love for each individual person. They always saw the reality of the cause, yet they did not despise the experience of the heart, of personal faith.

Later, the sick were healed without the laying-on of hands. 'If people expect a magic effect from the laying-on of hands, then let them be healed when I only preach.' The healing of faith remained.

The children loved Blumhardt very much. He gathered them around him daily and blessed them, laying his hands on them. The children could not misunderstand this.

9. *The Meaning of "Inner Light" and "God's Spirit"*

At the end of this section IV we would like to share what Eberhard Arnold said in answer to questions from guests on October 13, 1935, at the Rhön Bruderhof, about the Throne of God, about the world of stars and angels, about the World Spirit and the Holy Spirit.

I have had to think about some of the things our guest B. said. So I came to think about how it is with the Spirit and with life. It was said that we do not really need to expect and ask for the Spirit from above, but that the Spirit is in each man in the depths of his innermost being (John 1:9). This is something to think and ponder about in the depth of our hearts.

A certain translation of the Bible says that the light illumines every man when he comes into this world. This is no doubt one side of the truth. It is true.

The light that shines in each human heart is of God; it is a very specific light. But this light could not be in each individual man if the same light were not in the whole universe and above the whole vast creation. The first thing is not that this light and this Spirit is in the individual man, but the first thing is that this light and this Spirit is everywhere. Therefore we must testify to both. We must say with the apostolic Spirit: "God's Spirit testifies to our spirit." (Rom. 8:16) Both things meet—the inward light in our hearts and the powerful events in God's mighty universe. And the other way round, we have to say that if in each one of us there were not something of this light, we could not grasp the light in the great events of God. We would not be able to see the sun if our eyes were not sun-like. The two belong together. And therefore Jesus said that a man has to be renewed as an individual so that he may grasp the all-embracing universal things. ("Unless a man has been born over again he cannot see the kingdom of God." John 3:3, NEB)

Man is body, soul, and spirit. The spirit is a human spirit and a divine Spirit. Man in the beginning was absolute Spirit, but this does not come to expression in every man. If we follow the development of man, we can see that it is not a real development of his understanding and feeling, but only of his spirit. Therefore no brotherhood is possible where man starts out only from the mind and not from the heart. The community must be one heart and one soul. We also acknowledge the heart.

B.: When we see the suffering and need of unemployment and the great world-judgment, I cannot see how this can be caused by a god; I think that men themselves make the suffering and the war.

EBERHARD: That is faith in man, to which you confess. What do you think of the great starlit heaven which is spread above us? For as far as we can understand, compared with this world of stars our planet earth is very small.

B.: I think we know very little about creation, both scientifically and spiritually.

EBERHARD: But we do have an idea, the same as children have.

B.: When we ask, "How did life come to this world?" we stand before a question we cannot answer.

EBERHARD: I want to try to speak about that. We cannot examine God; that is not possible. So let us be more modest and look at our idea of the star-world and ask ourselves if God's Spirit and the human spirit are almost the same kind. When we see the great, starlit sky it is impossible to say that the human spirit and God's Spirit are of the same kind. Does this world of stars have less to do with a Spirit than man? Why should the world of stars have less to do with the Spirit than man has? Why should only we small human beings have a spirit? I would like to say this: we cannot examine God, but we can have an idea of the greatness of the universe and a feeling for it. Then we shall no longer think that man is so great, as though *he* were a god. I do not want to prove the existence of God, but we should feel a wonder before the universe, before the creation made by God Almighty. We can only speak about these divine things out of our experience. We cannot prove anything. No man can convince another through clever words; it is only to be grasped through experience. In the Sermon on the Mount there is the prayer to God in which God is addressed as the Father and in which God is asked that His will be done, that His Kingdom come to this world, and that man and the whole world may be delivered from evil. The Sermon on the Mount speaks of the Kingdom of God.

There are very deep mysteries. I have the feeling that in this way the truth can be sensed and perceived. I do not want to declare that what I say is absolutely true. Our human words are not enough to express all that we are now inwardly struggling to see.

It is very important to recognize the Spirit of the World on this earth. And in answer to the question whether war comes from men or from God, one could ask whether it does not come from the World-Spirit. I want to speak in a way that can be understood. Every planet has without doubt received a different angel-prince; Mars quite a different one from Venus; Saturn quite a different one from Neptune; the sun quite a different one from the planets, for the sun is a fire-system as no planet is. Its angel-prince can only be an angel of fire, such as we do not know on the earth or on the planets.

Every organism, all that has been created, has something of a soul, a spirit, a life-feeling. There is nothing that is only matter. What I say here is age-old wisdom, which has existed for many thousands of years among men. Therefore in the Old Testament and among the Babylonians, God is called the God of the angel-princes of the planets. And the Throne of God is represented in prophetic language as the entire world of stars. Therefore this Throne is likened to rolling wheels and to eyes of Heaven. This is the starlit sky. In this sky we can sense something of God and of God's Kingdom. Thus prophetic writings of all ages and the Revelation of John tell us that the Kingdom of God is certainly in our hearts, in our midst, but at the same time His Throne is in the world of stars. Jesus says that the Kingdom of God shall come to the earth, and at the same time He calls it the Kingdom of the Heavens. When Jesus speaks of the Kingdom of God in Heaven and on earth, that means that it shall come from Heaven down to earth. He is saying that God rules in the Heavens; on earth He does not rule yet. That is why He said, "Thy will be done on earth as it is in Heaven! Thy Kingdom come to this earth!"

POSTSCRIPT

This volume can be nothing more than an introduction to how Eberhard and Emmy Arnold with Else von Hollander and others were led to a life in community at Sannerz and on the Rhön in 1920. In sharing it, we ask that through the mercy of God all hearts everywhere may be moved toward a loving relationship to one another.

In future publications we hope to cover the whole Bruderhof story, supplementing Emmy Arnold's Bruderhof history.[1] A book in German is already in course of preparation and will be published in Germany. It will also be published in English.

After Eberhard Arnold's return from America in May 1931, the Rhön Bruderhof experienced an intensive time of inner awakening and deepening and of outer growth, doubling its numbers in the following four and a half years. The uniting with the Brothers called Hutterians was a real blessing and a source of new strength.

However, Adolf Hitler's rise to power in Germany in January 1933 brought many adversities to the community. The

---

[1] Emmy Arnold, *Torches Together: The Beginning and Early Years of the Bruderhof Communities*, 2nd ed. (Rifton, New York: Plough Publishing House, 1971).

pressure his National-Socialist government brought to bear on this small group of Christians and the restrictions it imposed on the Bruderhof (prohibiting the community to have an open door for seeking guests, closing the Bruderhof school, and refusing to exempt its young men from compulsory military service on grounds of their conscientious objection to any service in the armed forces) resulted in the founding of the Alm Bruderhof in Liechtenstein in the spring of 1934. Here the community school and the brothers of military age found refuge, and guests could visit freely again.

Apart from much economic deprivation, the enforced division of the small and as yet untested community brought much inner need to the whole circle in both places, particularly to Eberhard and Emmy Arnold; they traveled constantly between the Rhön and the Alm for the next one and a half years in a loving attempt to help both communities in this distressing situation.

In spite of their efforts and those of some other members, a spirit of moralism and later one of cold officialdom and work efficiency, coming from a strong urge for power over brothers and sisters, developed on the Alm Bruderhof among the leading brothers in 1934 and 1935. Eberhard fought this with inner fire, authority, and love, and the circle seemed to respond. Soon afterwards, however, a similar if not worse situation arose on the mother Bruderhof: a narrow-minded, petty spirit of religious self-centeredness, emotional sympathy and antipathy (leading to cliquishness and gossip), human democracy, vacillation, and tolerance of evil spread among the members on the Rhön; it threatened to drive out the good Spirit and to disintegrate the community from within. In spite of protests arising from the circle itself and Eberhard's and Emmy's determined and loving struggle for a radical turning around, this complete opposition to the Living Spirit continued.

Finally, when the Brotherhood in Germany—deprived of so many devoted members who had left for Liechtenstein— ceased to function as a living, fighting community organism, it placed itself under the discipline of the Brotherhood on the Alm Bruderhof. The Alm Brotherhood hoped that through this serious step and through the help of several brothers and sisters sent from the Alm to the Rhön Bruderhof, the circle there would experience a completely new beginning. They hoped that the sullen, dull resistance and the lovelessness prevalent on the Rhön would make room for the spirit of repentance, leading to a new, joyful dedication, a new love, and a deep concern for world suffering and the greatness of God's redemption in Jesus for men, for the earth, and for the whole vast universe.

It was at the beginning of November 1935, in this very painful situation, that Eberhard Arnold traveled from the Rhön Bruderhof to Darmstadt (Hesse) to undergo surgery on his right leg. Two years earlier, on his return from the city of Kassel after a very difficult encounter with the Gestapo, he had slipped and fallen on a wet slope close to the Rhön Bruderhof and broken his leg. The complicated fracture had never healed properly. Yet Eberhard had not spared himself in the least but had traveled extensively between the two Bruderhofs and in Europe with much discomfort and pain, risking a collapse of the broken leg at any moment.

It was here in Darmstadt, away from his beloved communities, that Eberhard died on November 22, 1935, in great physical need and anguish of soul but in complete faith in God and submission to His will and in burning love to Jesus. An unsuccessful operation on November 16 had made the amputation of the broken leg necessary. Eberhard died after this second operation. Only Emmy, his beloved wife, and her sister Monika Barth were at his side during the last difficult days, until at the very last moment Eberhard's eldest daughter Emi-Margret and her husband arrived from Liechtenstein. Eberhard Arnold died a lonely death, without the inner support of the communities that owed their very existence more to his seeking, fighting, calling, and gathering than to that of any other man.

The Brotherhood needed to repent deeply for their coldness and lethargy, and for their opposition to the Spirit of Jesus, which had spoken to them so clearly through the prophetic voice of Eberhard. How he had suffered from the enforced division, the lack of response to his warnings, and the lovelessness that threatened to destroy the community from within during the last eighteen months of his life! It seems unbelievable that there was no united Brotherhood at the Rhön Bruderhof when Eberhard died, no believing, fighting circle to stand by him. After this catastrophe, only deep remorse and genuine repentance could save the communities from utter ruin.

That the Bruderhof survived at all is a real miracle of God. However, the inner disloyalty of 1934–1935 was so deep-rooted that true repentance was given only after years, even decades of long-drawn-out struggles. The stubborn, often hidden resistance to the Spirit, the Spirit of love and unity, had taken a strong foothold in the communities, particularly in those members entrusted with the leadership of the Bruder-hofs. This resistance was demonic in character and amounted to an outright rejection of Eberhard and his widow Emmy Arnold and the way of discipleship of Jesus they had represented to the last. It was utterly evil.

Several attempts to fight for a breakthrough of the true Spirit of discipleship against this evil were of no avail. The arrogant communitarianism based on human principles and human power prevailed right through the late thirties to the forties and fifties. The switch points were set wrongly, and the train was rushing headlong in the wrong direction toward the abyss.

Nevertheless, the community grew in numbers as it still attracted seeking people. The Bruderhof in Germany was dissolved by the Nazis in 1937, and the Alm Bruderhof was given up in 1938, all its members moving to the Cotswold Bruderhof in England. In the long, difficult years that followed, the Bruderhof spread from England to Paraguay and after the Second World War to Uruguay, to Germany (again), and to the United States.

In spite of the wrong direction the Bruderhof was taking, there was a hidden seed of renewal at work. Without it the communities would have foundered; but there were members who tried to hold to what they knew to be right even though their efforts to let the Spirit of Jesus triumph were ignored and rejected.

It belongs to the miracle of this survival that in the midst of spiritual deterioration the Bruderhof movement experienced now and then brief periods, in one or the other of its communities, of a greater sense of inner freedom and joy, a truer sense of dedication and mission. These were bright interludes in those otherwise so sad, drab, and unmoved years. They meant hope and encouragement for the deeply perturbed older members as well as for those young in the fight. This was true in the early days (late thirties) of the Cotswold Bruderhof in England; in Paraguay in 1941 and later; at the founding of the Wheathill Bruderhof in England in 1942; and most forcefully at the founding of the Woodcrest Bruderhof in North America in 1954.

This new community in the State of New York came into being because the Primavera Brotherhood in Paraguay in its longing for outreach and renewal had sent members on mission to the United States in the late forties and early fifties. They found a longing for community there, which had crystallized in several serious attempts at community living, such as Koinonia and Macedonia in Georgia, Kingwood in New Jersey, and several community groups in California. The brothers and sisters from Paraguay were warmly received by these groups.

Several members of these community ventures, together with people from Quaker and Brethren and other backgrounds, joined with the brothers in establishing a new Bruderhof community at Woodcrest in 1954. The uniting power and basis for this community was Jesus Christ. Though a stumbling block for some who turned away, this decisive witness drew many to Woodcrest, and the community grew rapidly.

In 1957 the remaining members of Macedonia Cooperative Community began to read the Gospel of Luke as part of a search for deeper unity among them. Out of this search, many of the members were struck in their hearts with an urge to follow Jesus and to found their community life completely on Him. In this new conviction they asked to unite with the Bruderhof, and this uniting took place in 1957 at Macedonia. After one year, Macedonia was closed and the community moved to Connecticut as the Evergreen Bruderhof. The Oak Lake Bruderhof was established also in 1957 in western Pennsylvania. Both these communities underwent inner struggles for the firm establishment of a truly Christian community life.

The spirit of joy, love, and freedom that prevailed in Woodcrest from the outset was never lost. The same can be said for Evergreen and New Meadow Run (formerly Oak Lake) after their initial struggles. It was from these small new beginnings that the whole Bruderhof movement eventually found a new birth, arising like a phoenix from the ashes. In all other instances the evil power so firmly entrenched in some members since 1934/35 spread its hold over all Bruderhofs. Again and again it destroyed any new beginning or effort towards a revival, sometimes just strangling it by sheer willful disregard, at other times nipping any such stirrings in the bud or simply crushing them outright.

Only because there were brothers and sisters in all communities longing to recapture the original spirit of love and freedom could the whole Bruderhof movement find new life again. It was their persistent, quiet faith and fervent longing that held the community together. It is a real miracle that in those difficult years new members joined from the circle of the grown-up children of the community families and from outside. Through the leading and protection of God, many new brothers and sisters joined in the early and mid-fifties, who in the fear of God began their life afresh, particularly on the Bruderhof in Woodcrest. (A few also joined in the communities in Europe and South America.)

These new brothers and sisters rejected all fear of men. They recognized that our deceased Word Leader Eberhard Arnold was a man of God. They sought to establish their bond in baptism on the rock foundation of God's *living* Word. In spite of much weakness, many errors, and even guilt, it was through these newly awakened and gathered brothers and sisters—who wanted to build up their lives on the foundation of the Word of God alone—that God gave us the grace of a new beginning.

In its attempt to destroy the communities from within, the divisive, evil power at work in the communities brought about a break with the Brothers known as Hutterians. This originated in Forest River, North Dakota, in 1955. At that time several members of this Hutterian colony were seeking a closer relationship with the Society of Brothers in Woodcrest. Some of the members of Forest River even felt strongly drawn to "join" the Society of Brothers. In the ensuing conflict with our Hutterian Brothers of Manitoba and South Dakota, brothers and sisters acted sinfully. We took possession of the Forest River Colony for a time. This was legally in order but it violated the love of the Sermon on the Mount. We accepted some of its members into membership of our own group, and in this way forced those members of Forest River who wanted to stay loyal to the Hutterian Brothers to leave their own colony. We deeply regret this arrogant act, which led to a complete break

with the Brothers called Hutterians. This break took more
than eighteen years to repair.

Jesus' Spirit does not tolerate being mixed with other spirits.
Either His Spirit withdraws or the other spirits must leave.
In the new beginning at Woodcrest, Jesus' living Spirit kindled
a fire of daily repentance and daily forgiveness. This quickened
the hope and faith of those old members who for years had
been seeking an inner renewal of what Eberhard and Emmy
Arnold, Else von Hollander, and others had been called to
give their lives for: the discipleship of Jesus. In the years
1959 to 1961, those who opposed the Gospel of repentance
and represented a human "communitarian" approach (among
whom were almost all the leading members in South America
and Europe) made various attempts to crush this new awakening, as similar awakenings had been crushed since 1935. During
the years 1960–1961 it came to a hard struggle between the
opposing spirits at work in the communities since the time of
Eberhard Arnold's death. It was a spiritual fight. Many members in all Bruderhofs, particularly in Woodcrest and in the
other new American communities, took up this fight against
all human power and fear of men, for they wanted to build
their lives on the fear of God alone. The fight was carried
out in the heart of every brother and sister and in the
Brotherhoods of each Bruderhof. It was a matter of finally
stopping the train and putting it on the right track to the
right destination again.

The struggle between the two opposing atmospheres was
intense and had serious and unforeseen consequences. It led
to giving up the Bruderhof settlements in South America and

Germany after they had virtually collapsed. Also the Wheat-hill Bruderhof in England had to be given up. At that time many members of the older Bruderhofs left the community, either on their own initiative or at the request of the members determined to continue a life of true brotherhood. The latter felt too weak to cope with those who resisted the longed-for renewal and who held on to the old, proud, and loveless ways, or with those who were in complete inner turmoil at the time and unable to be of help in this most difficult crisis situation. Many of those who left the communities have already returned and are in the Bruderhofs as fully united brothers and sisters. It was in those critical years—and still is now—the hope and longing of the Brotherhood in all Bruderhof communities that *all* former members, originally called to this way by Jesus, will find a completely new beginning again with all of us in a renewed brotherly life.

A serious attempt was made in 1964 to repair the break with the Hutterian Brothers that followed the Forest River affair in 1955, and there was some friendly mutual visiting as a result of these efforts. By pleading for forgiveness for the wrong done to the Brothers and accepting discipline, a complete reconciliation and new unity between the two groups was given in January–February of 1974. We were able thus, together, to start all over again where Eberhard Arnold left off in 1935. We are deeply thankful that this reuniting came about through Eberhard and Emmy's son Heini, who has been serving the communities as our Elder since 1962 in the same Spirit of humility, love, and clarity which brought us together in the beginning and led us to the Brothers in 1930 and again in 1974.

The three Bruderhof communities in the Eastern United States and the one in England[2] stand united in Spirit with a keen sense of mutual help and of inner and practical working together with *all* Bruderhofs, East or West. All their members are committed to fight for a genuine life of joyful obedience and surrender to God, of love to Jesus and to all brothers and sisters everywhere. There is a great longing that God's Spirit will lead all the communities of the Brothers known as Hutterians, old or new, to true mission again and to the gathering of men for Jesus and His Kingdom. Such mission or outreach can only be given on the basis of our realizing our own smallness before God's greatness and majesty. It is to His honor and praise alone that everything we do should be done. We owe everything to Him, to His grace, love, compassion, and mercy.

The urge to mission and gathering is at work among us also because we feel that God's judgment and His Kingdom are close at hand. It is so very evident today that love is waxing cold, and sin and evil are on the increase everywhere in the world in truly frightening proportions.

In conclusion we must say, with our departed Word Leader Eberhard Arnold,[3] what the apostles of Jesus Christ testify concerning the Holy Spirit: "God's Spirit bears witness with our spirit." (Rom. 8:16) We ask for ourselves and for all zealous souls that the greatness of God and of His and our

[2] Woodcrest, Rifton, New York; Evergreen, Norfolk, Connecticut; New Meadow Run, Farmington, Pennsylvania; and Darvell, Robertsbridge, Sussex, England.

[3] See section 9 of the last chapter.

Jesus Christ and of His Holy Spirit may live in our hearts and that the light of the Kingdom of God may be active and alive in us.

We can see the Kingdom of God only when we have been born again through faith in Jesus Christ. So it is our prayer that God the Almighty, the Father of Jesus Christ, who is our Father too, may come to rule also on this earth. Jesus asks for His will to be done here on earth as in Heaven. So we stand before the mystery of the greatness of God and the greatness of Jesus Christ, who from the Father has received authority over all angel-powers, spirits, and principalities.

Hardy Arnold